UNLEASHING
The Gift of Giving

A Ministry's Guide to Building and Leaving a Legacy

Andrew —
Thank you for your transformational
work in the body of Christ!

For the
Kingdom

Rusty Russell, CFP®

Rusty

Disclaimer: All of the assumptions, examples, etc. in this book are for illustration purposes only. All of the information contained in this book is believed to be true and accurate at the time of publication. At the time of publication, the Economic Growth And Tax Relief Reconciliation Act of 2001, which had been partially extended from 2010 to 2012, is set to expire. Unless stated otherwise, all tax rates used are based on 2013 assumptions. Tax and estate law changes over time and varies from state to state. Each person's circumstances are unique and will vary from the illustrations contained herein. Nothing in this book should be considered as specific financial, tax, or legal advice. As with all broadly-written advice, consult with your financial, tax, and legal advisors.

All scripture references are King James Version unless indicated otherwise.

ISBN: 978-1-936750-67-2

TABLE OF CONTENTS

Acknowledgements

Thank you to my wife, Michele, my blessing, whose faith in me has encouraged me in countless ways. You have prayed, cried, and pressed with me as we have unleashed the gift of giving in our own lives, and without your fervent and steadfast support, I would not be the man I am today.

Thank you to my children, Robby, Matt, Isaac, and Elizabeth. You are living examples of those who are quick to give to the Lord and to others, each in your own unique ways, out of your substance, your time, your effort, and your heart. I am so excited to see each of you walking in the things God has prepared for you in your own special calling.

Thank you to Donna Parsons, my assistant, my co-laborer, the one who never does merely her best, but always does whatever it takes. You have captured and carried the vision of this book, both at the office and in prayer. Without your dedication, this book could not have happened.

Thank you to my pastor, J. B. Whitfield. Your hope, joy, and unwavering commitment to imparting the principles of the Word of God have made a positive difference in my life and family in countless ways.

I also owe gratitude to my original mentor on giving: the late Johnny Simmons. It was his ministry of the Word of God that first opened my eyes to the gift of giving. I will never forget him or his legacy that so impacted my life.

Unleashing the Gift of Giving:

Dedication

I dedicate this discourse on giving to the one who tirelessly gave of herself to her family and her Lord, my mother, the late Jean Russell. One of Mom's missions in life was to work to have to give to her children so that they could have a better life. Not only did Mom give to us material things, but a rich heritage of faith in God and love for others, especially those less fortunate than us. I miss her deeply but know that I will see her again when I am finished with my assignment on this earth.

> *"We always thank God, the Father of our Lord Jesus Christ, when we pray for you. We thank him because we have heard about your faith in Christ Jesus. We have also heard that you love all of God's people. Your faith and love are based on the hope you have. What you hope for is stored up for you in heaven. You have already heard about it. You were told about it when the message of truth was given to you. I'm talking about the good news that has come to you. All over the world the good news is bearing fruit and growing. It has been doing that among you since the day you heard it. That is when you understood God's grace in all its truth."*
>
> Colossians 1:3-6 (NIrV)

Unleashing the Gift of Giving:

Preface

For several weeks in early 2006, I had been sensing the Lord nudging me to write a book about legacy planning. I did not have a specific direction, but more of a gentle preparation. As I prayed about it, I became more sure that this book was to be a book for ministries, to help them work with people who had the gift of giving in order for both the ministry and the giver to achieve God's will for their life, each doing their own part in ministry.

In July of 2006, I met with my pastor for breakfast to discuss writing the book. After that meeting, I was meditating on our conversation. I had been working on options for the book, but did not have clarity on the title. While sitting in my car, I heard these words come roaring up out of my spirit: "UNLEASHING THE GIFT OF GIVING!" It was so strong and so loud on the inside of me that it startled me. I immediately wrote it down and then began to meditate on what the Lord was trying to say. I saw how so many believers had been given the gift of giving and called to fund the kingdom of God, but did not know where to begin, both spiritually and practically. The gift of giving was being held back like a dog on a leash. The gift of giving is ready to run and bring wealth in to the kingdom of God; all that is needed is to remove the leash! This book is not about ways to get money to fund a ministry; this book is about how to unleash the gift of giving already surging on the inside of believers who are called to fund the kingdom of God, which, in turn, will get the necessary resources to ministries.

Now that I had the title, I just had to write the book. I knew this book was something the Lord had been stirring on the inside of me, and thought I knew how to proceed. I had the technical and spiritual background, I had a desire to communicate about God's ability to provide every need, but something was missing—the why. Although I could draw several mental conclusions, I still did not have a full understanding of His purpose. A few weeks later during a Sunday morning service, I was not even thinking about writing this book, and had actually set it aside while I was busy with other things. Suddenly, I heard the Spirit of the Lord almost shout inside my spirit, "WRITE THE BOOK! I HAVE NEED OF IT!" Suddenly, I had the why; I had the motivation. I no longer had merely a "God idea"—I had a mandate. I thought about the colt tied up that the disciples brought for Jesus to ride into Jerusalem, the colt that ushered in the New Covenant. I realized this book was not about me, this book was not about others, this book was about Him. He has need of it.

This book is written for ministers—those charged with the financial and spiritual growth of a ministry. As a minister, you may have an administrative staff to handle the details, but you are the one accountable to God for the administration and growth of your ministry. As you read this book, do not read it for information only. Allow it to minister to you, not just educate you. This is a last-days message. He has need of it. May the Spirit of God Himself anoint your ears to hear what the Spirit would say to the church. Amen.

Chapter 1

Why Unleash the Gift of Giving?

Motives and Intents of the Heart

*A good man leaves an inheritance to his
children's children....*

Proverbs 13:22

A legacy is a gift or inheritance left to an heir. It is what
you pass to the next generation that will represent you when
you are gone.

**A successful legacy is best achieved by the skillful
blending of the work of the ministry with the wealth of
the giver around a common vision.** In order to have a successful legacy, a ministry needs sufficient resources to pass
its vision to the ministry's successor. A family needs to pass
meaning and significance along with their wealth to the next
generation to have a successful legacy. These needs serve as
the catalyst to begin the legacy planning process. Combining
these two legacy needs creates dynamic opportunities for
success for both the ministry and the giver.

Motive

Why do you want to leave a legacy? Why do you want to unleash the gift of giving? What is your reason, your motive?

Whatever your reason, it will fall into one of two categories: to further the Kingdom of God or to further your own aspirations. I do not mean to say that desiring to increase and grow and flourish is an ungodly thing—quite the opposite! God desires that we be

The real question is, "Whose agenda will this growth fulfill: His or yours?

fruitful and multiply and fill up the earth with all that He has in store for us. Maybe you are at the beginning stages of your ministry and you are just hoping to make it to next month and keep the lights on. Maybe your goal is to continue to grow your well-established ministry for generations to come.

The real question is, "Whose agenda will this growth fulfill: His or yours?" If you intend to use this book to find a better way to meet your own needs by getting others to give to you, stop now! Of course it may seem so clear that your ministry is for God, about God, and founded at the direction of God. Dig deeper. Make sure you are really clear about the desire of your heart. Jeremiah warns us that, "The heart is deceitful above all things, and desperately wicked; who can know it? I, the LORD, search the heart…" (Jeremiah 17:9-10).

Ask the Lord, right now, to show you what is truly in your heart. If it is truly to further His kingdom, His way of doing things—great! Read on! But, if you are even the least bit unsure of the purity of your motive, either from fear or immaturity or whatever, stop now and seek full understanding of His plans for the future of your ministry. "If any of you lacks wisdom, let him ask of God, who gives to all liberally and without reproach, and it will be given to him. But let him ask in faith, with no doubting, for he who doubts is like a wave of the sea driven and tossed by the wind. For let not that man suppose that he will receive anything from the Lord; *he is* a double-minded man, unstable in all his ways" (James 1:5-8). God desires for you to know His plans for you, your future, and the future of your ministry. If after you can say, in faith, that you are sure that your desire is to further His kingdom, read on and Unleash the Gift of Giving!

Further the Kingdom of God.

That sounds simple enough, but maybe too simple, too vague. How does a ministry further the kingdom of God concerning giving? By ministering giving. Again, that sounds simple, but vague. How do we "minister" giving? By teaching sound doctrine on giving, operating the finances of the ministry according to that doctrine, and ministering to the giver, both the giver of current gifts and the giver of planned gifts (more on that later.)

When you focus the financial aspect of your ministry on ministering to the giver, not just receiving from the giver, you work as a co-laborer with the giver to build a lasting legacy of ministry with integrity. This, in turn, furthers the laws of the Kingdom of God operating in the ministry *and* in the giver, thereby both increasing in the fruit of righteousness and leaving their own legacy for the generations to come. That is unleashing the gift of giving.

For too long, the gift of giving has been restrained: restrained by religious tradition, restrained by fear, restrained by ignorance, restrained by selfishness, and many other ungodly restraints. Trust God that, as you delve into the material in this book, He will give you a clear revelation of how to keep from restraining His gift of giving in your ministry and in those to whom you minister so you can build a legacy for the Kingdom of God.

The Need to Create a Ministry Legacy

Since motive is such a big deal, why should anyone build a legacy anyhow? Does God really need our help furthering His kingdom? Absolutely! We are the body of Christ. We are the laborers. We are all He has to work with on this earth. Remember again God's blessing for man spoken to Adam: "Be fruitful and multiply; fill the earth and subdue it; have dominion…" (Genesis 1:28). That is our job. Create a legacy. In fact, fill the whole earth with all that God made that was good. Now that is a legacy! Unfortunately, our world today is woefully short of fulfilling our mandate to leave a legacy for God, but that is one reason why it is all the more important.

Does God really need our help furthering His kingdom? Absolutely!

In Luke 19, Zacchaeus makes his famous pledge to the Lord that he will unleash the gift of giving, giving half of his goods to the poor and paying back four times anything he has taken through cheating. Just after that, Jesus tells us the story of the nobleman's journey.

> *[11]Now as they heard these things, He spoke another parable, because He was near Jerusalem and because they thought the kingdom of God would appear immediately. [12]Therefore He said: "A certain nobleman went into a far country to receive for himself a kingdom and to return. [13]So he called ten of his servants, delivered to them ten minas, and said to them, 'Do business till I come.' [14]But his citizens hated him, and sent a delegation after him, saying, 'We will not have this man to reign over us.'*
>
> *[15]"And so it was that when he returned, having received the kingdom, he then commanded these servants, to whom he had given the money, to be called to him, that he might know how much every man had gained by trading. [16]Then came the first, saying, 'Master, your mina has earned ten minas.' [17]And he said to him, 'Well done, good servant; because you were faithful in a very little, have authority over ten cities.' [18]And the second came, saying, 'Master, your mina has earned five minas.' [19]Likewise he said to him, 'You also be over five cities.'*
>
> *[20]"Then another came, saying, 'Master, here is your mina, which I have kept put away in a handkerchief. [21]For I feared you, because you are an austere man. You collect what you did not deposit, and reap what you*

*did not sow.' [22]And he said to him, 'Out of
your own mouth I will judge you, you wicked
servant. You knew that I was an austere man,
collecting what I did not deposit and reaping
what I did not sow. [23]Why then did you not
put my money in the bank, that at my coming
I might have collected it with interest?'*
     *[24]"And he said to those who stood by,
'Take the mina from him, and give it to him
who has ten minas.' [25](But they said to him,
'Master, he has ten minas.') [26]'For I say to
you, that to everyone who has will be given;
and from him who does not have, even what he
has will be taken away from him. [27]But bring
here those enemies of mine, who did not want
me to reign over them, and slay them before
me.'"*

                                     Luke 19:11-27 (NKJV)

In the King James version, verse 13 uses the word
"occupy," but the actual meaning of that word is to do business, continue growing assets, expanding. We see this in
the rewards given to the servants upon the master's return.
Whether we own and operate a for-profit business, lead and
direct a ministry, or work for an employer, we are expected
to grow assets, expand capability, and advance. Jesus said,
"And from the days of John the Baptist until the present
time, the kingdom of heaven has endured violent assault,
and violent men seize it by force [as a precious prize–a
share in the heavenly kingdom is sought with most ardent
zeal and intense exertion]." (Matt 11:12 Amplified). From
God the Father's original job description given to man to be
fruitful and multiply to the transfer of the ministry of Jesus,

exhorting those that would come after Him to follow in his legacy and do greater works than He (John 14:12).

God is all about increase. We who are called into His ministry, whether in the five-fold ministry of pastor, evangelist, apostle, prophet, or teacher, or in business or government, we are to be about increasing and leaving a legacy. It is not an option; it is a command. The only question that remains is how will we handle this charge He has left to us—hiding it idly out of laziness and fear or working to increase it according to our ability, bringing increase and hearing the Master say, "Well done, good and faithful servant. You were faithful over a few things, I will make you ruler over many things. Enter into the joy of your Lord." The choice is ours.

Chapter 2

What is the Gift of Giving?

Who and How

You will be made rich in every way so that you can be generous on every occasion, and through us your generosity will result in thanksgiving to God.

II Corinthians 9:11 (NIV)

Who Has the Gift of Giving?

One of the things every believer is called to do is give. We are told to give all throughout the Bible, Old and New Testament alike. Every born-again believer has the ability and corresponding responsibility to be a giver. First, in Malachi 3:10, we are instructed in the tithe, the connection to our covenant. After that, we are to give offerings, give to the poor, and take care of the widow, orphan and stranger. In other words, we are to give to what the world refers to as charity, which is another word for love. This is modeled by God Himself, as He so loved the world He gave. We who are created in His image are to be His representatives of giving on the earth, helping Him to meet needs.

Just as some people are called to be pastors or evangelists, there are those who are called by God to be givers—those with the gift of giving. Those whose very talents and desires, submitted to God's plan, long to finance the spreading of the kingdom of God, whether through humanitarian relief of food, clothing, and shelter; evangelism; education; medical; or other deliverables that advance the kingdom of God in the earth.

Paul, in his first letter to Timothy, has a charge for those who are wealthy: "Command those who are rich in this present age not to be haughty, nor trust in uncertain riches but in the living God, who gives us richly all things to enjoy. Let them do good, that they be rich in good works, ready to give, willing to share, storing up for themselves a good foundation for the time to come, that they may lay hold on eternal life." (I Tim 6:17-19) Most of the sixth chapter gives instructions on how to handle

Unfortunately, too many who are wealthy have been taught that they should not be wealthy, and that somehow God is unhappy with their wealth.

wealth. Unfortunately, through misunderstanding or intentional misapplication, too many who are wealthy have been taught that they should not be wealthy, and that somehow God is unhappy with their wealth. Nothing could be further from the truth. If you carefully study chapter 6, you will see that Paul is not attacking wealth, but greed.

Those who lustfully pursue wealth to fund their own desires are practicing a form of idolatry: the love of money. Those who pursue financial gain to meet the needs of the kingdom of God are pursuing righteousness, godliness, faith, love, patience, and gentleness. Money does not corrupt motives; it merely reveals motives by amplifying the ability to act on motives. The one with the gift of giving is constantly looking for opportunities to meet the needs of others to bring glory to God. Being wealthy for God is the embodiment of the gift of giving and is exemplified in II Corinthians 9:6-8:

> "⁶[Remember] this: he who sows sparingly and grudgingly will also reap sparingly and grudgingly, and he who sows generously [that blessings may come to someone] will also reap generously and with blessings. ⁷Let each one [give] as he has made up his own mind and purposed in his heart, not reluctantly or sorrowfully or under compulsion, for God loves (He takes pleasure in, prizes above other things, and is unwilling to abandon or to do without) a cheerful (joyous, 'prompt to do it') giver [whose heart is in his giving]. ⁸And God is able to make all grace (every favor and earthly blessing) come to you in abundance, so that you may always and under all circumstances and whatever the need be self-sufficient [possessing enough to require no aid or support and furnished in abundance for every good work and charitable donation]."
>
> (Amplified)

The one who has the gift of giving is quick to give and will be supplied to give more. That is the whole purpose for the process of giving and receiving—to have more to give. That is the gift of giving.

The Bible is full of examples of those with the gift of giving. Elisha's ministry was furthered by a woman, a non-Jewish Gentile, who had the gift of giving. In II Kings 4, the wealthy woman in Shunem began by feeding Elisha and his servant, Gehazi. After a while, she had her husband build an extra room onto their home to give Elisha a place to rest when he traveled by. As a result of her giving to meet the needs of Elisha, the prophet of God, God gave this barren woman a son. Later, when her son died of a fever, God raised him back to life.

Similarly, in the New Testament, a wealthy woman in Joppa, a Greek disciple named Dorcas, was well known for "abounding in good deeds and acts of charity" (Acts 9:36 Amplified). She became sick and died. When Peter got word of this, he came to Joppa, went to her room, prayed, and spoke to her body and commanded it to get up. She did. This miracle was a sign to people all around Joppa and many became believers as a result.

In Acts chapter 10, Cornelius, a Gentile and captain of the Italian Regiment, was a devout man who revered God and gave charitable gifts to the people and prayed to God continually. During a time of prayer, Cornelius was visited by an angel who told him that his prayers and his donations to the poor were known to God. As a result, He sent Peter to preach the Gospel to Cornelius, the first Gentile believer to receive the Holy Spirit.

In Acts 11, when Paul and Barnabus were in Antioch, a famine came upon the earth. The disciples at Antioch "resolved to send relief, each according to his individual ability [in proportion as he had prospered], to the brethren who lived in Judea. And so they did, sending [their contributions] to the elders by the hand of Barnabas and Saul" (Acts 11:29-30 Amplified).

These are just a few examples of God working through His people to meet the needs of the world, especially the household of faith.

THE STORY

Nathan and Eva Wright are frustrated. They have always been committed to God, their church, their family, and one another. During their forty years of marriage, they have had a good life, a very good life. Nathan has been very successful in business and Eva has stayed involved in their community, helping wherever there was a need. Still, there's one thing that keeps bothering them—they're rich. That may sound silly to most people, but not to them. They see their financial resources as a curse more than a blessing. Yes, they are glad they can use their financial resources to help meet needs, but they somehow feel like God disapproves of them because they are wealthy.

When they were younger and just starting out, they had lots of friends. Everyone seemed to get along well with one another and were always quick to help one another out when they needed it, even if it was just an ear to listen or a shoulder to cry on. Now that they are in their late fifties, "have arrived" and are quite financially secure, it seems that those friendships seem to have stayed in the past. It is almost like their old friends are are uncomfortable around them just because they now have money.

> Nathan and Eva have spent many nights wishing they could return to the time when their friends needed them, not just their money. Now most friendships are related in some way to getting money, not directly, but for a good cause, a need in the community, in the church, or in another part of the world. Their days of purposeful relationships have been relegated to an impersonal and utilitarian writing of checks to "help" someone they do not even know.

How is the Gift of Giving Tied Up?

If we are to unleash the gift of giving, then it must be tied up somehow. How could that happen? Many years ago, my pastor was praying for God to send in the harvest to the church – the lives that would be brought into the kingdom of God. After a time of praying, walking back and forth across the front of the church, he heard the voice of the Lord in what seemed like an audible voice say, "I cannot send the harvest." He replied, "Why not?" The Lord answered, "Because you do not have people trained to disciple the harvest."

From that time until now, our church has developed methods, systems, and processes to disciple the harvest, training members to minister to the harvest. The process begins when a first-time attender arrives in the parking lot and attends their first church service. The ongoing discipleship includes a training course for a new believer and a comprehensive new member class that helps them understand church doctrine, how to handle offense, how to relate to spiritual authority, and discovering and unwrapping their gifts. When they graduate from the new members class, they enter church membership and become a minister to the harvest – and so the cycle repeats and grows.

The methods, systems, and processes are to make sure that nothing is left undone and that everything is done in excellence. Now that we have people trained to disciple the harvest, we have surely seen increase in every area of our church, not just numerically, but in levels of maturity and outreach.

Why would anyone in ministry believe that it would be any different with God's harvest of wealth—the great wealth transfer? So many ministers and ministries are crying out for the harvest of wealth to accomplish the mandates given to them by God, but they do not have the methods, systems, and processes to disciple (make disciplined application of) the harvest—the individuals with the wealth and the wealth itself. The Bible says in Haggai 1:7, "Consider your ways."

> *By much learning the rooms are filled with all riches that are pleasing and of great worth.*
> *Proverbs 24:4 (NLV)*

So why is the gift of giving tied up? Just like an imma- ture and undisciplined dog, it must be leashed since it is not trained to be a blessing to its master. If you have ever owned a puppy, you know that an immature and untrained dog chews, digs, and destroys property. Left untrained, this destructive puppy grows to be a very big destructive dog. However, the mature, well-trained dog is in tune with his master, yielding to his every command, serving the master in whatever the master desires. The gift of giving, like the dog, can be a blessing or a terror depending on how it is mastered. Just like the dog, it is not the fault of the gift of giving when things go wrong; it is the fault of the master. How you choose to master the harvest of wealth through the gift of giving will determine if it can be unleashed in your ministry and life. It is a decision. It is a process. It is essential to achieve all that God has called you to do.

The learning begins with knowledge. Many Christians are familiar with the first line of Hosea 4:6, "My people are destroyed for lack of knowledge." But the whole verse is very telling:

> *My people are destroyed for lack of knowledge. Because you have rejected knowledge, I also will reject you from being priest for Me; because you have forgotten the law of your God, I also will forget your children.*
> *Hosea 4:6 (NKJV)*

Absence of knowledge of God's way of doing things can lead to destruction: destruction of ministries, vision, and legacy. But not just what you do not know, but also what you may know that you reject or forget. Knowing the right things to do is not enough. You must also act on what you know. Often fear, distrust, greed, and other negative motivators can lead to a rejection and forgetting what one knows they ought to do. Not doing what is right concerning building and leaving a legacy can leash the very gift of giving vital to building and leaving the legacy.

This book will give you the knowledge to begin developing the methods, systems and processes to unleash the gift of giving. This book will not give you all of the answers, many of which are unique to your ministry and the mandates that God has given to you. This book will serve as a tool to educate and motivate you to develop those methods, systems, and processes so that you can disciple the wealthy and the wealth.

How to Unleash the Gift of Giving

But without faith it is impossible to please
Him, for he who comes to God must believe
that He is, and that He is a rewarder of those
who diligently seek Him.
Hebrews 11:6 (NKJV)

Before the gift of giving can operate in its effective working, it must be unleashed. There are several ways to unleash the giving. Here are a few.

Minister the Word on Giving to the Giver

Although this may seem obvious, many givers are not firmly grounded in what the Bible teaches about money and perish from lack of knowledge. As a result, many deal with fear when faced with opportunities to give. Often it is out of fear of not having enough left over, that somehow giving in response to God's direction will lead to poverty. Sometimes it is out of a lack of a developed ability to hear what God is instructing, and that maybe they are acting on their own accord or on a deception of the devil. Sometimes there is even a concern for appearance, not wanting anyone to think that they are trying to flaunt their wealth for status or fame—this is an affront to the one with the gift of giving. Whatever the hesitancy, it often stems from a lack of clear understanding of Biblical finance—what God really says about money and giving.

Unfortunately, this lack of understanding is compounded by the hesitancy of many ministries to teach on Biblical finance, especially giving. Many ministers fear that if they teach on giving and encourage people to give, it will be perceived as manipulative and pushy, and will drive money away instead of free the gift of giving. Remember the section on motive at the beginning of the book? If it is the motive of a ministry to use teaching on giving in order to get money, it will drive away the gift of giving. If it is the motive of a ministry to minister to the giver by teaching on giving, it will facilitate the gift of giving to operate freely. So, out of fear of offending the giver, the ministry has, in effect, done a great disservice to the giver, leashing the gift of giving. The wealthy believer needs for ministries to minister the Word of God on giving with a pure and clear heart and a pure and clear message, with just as much passion as a message on salvation or holiness.

Be Aware of the Heart of the Giver

The wealthy believer needs discipleship in his or her gifting just as much as anyone else does in their gifting. They also need to be held accountable. If you teach them the truth, they will be discipled. Also, just like anyone else, respect them and their confidentiality as they mature in their gifting. Also, never lose sight that it is God, giving through the giver, that is the ministry's source; the giver is never the source. Just as much as fear can completely destroy this necessary discipleship, proper discipleship in the word of God ministered in the love of God can destroy fear.

Some ministries are unable to teach a message on giving because they are in bondage to poor people with money, those people who use their money to control and manipulate. This is not the heart of the gift of giving. This kind of giving is ungodly, and is not giving at all, but a form of spiritual extortion. Out of fear that God will not meet the needs of the ministry, many ministers continue being manipulated and controlled by ungodly people with money. Do not be like the wicked and fearful servant with what He has entrusted to you. If you are in that situation, be encouraged that you are not alone, but be exhorted to stop, repent, put your trust in the Lord, and give Him back control of His ministry that He has entrusted to you.

Provide Practical Solutions to the Giver

Just as much as people can perish for a lack of knowledge of concepts, they can perish just as easily for a lack of practical steps to implement those concepts. When approached by a giver, be ready with your ministry's vision, projects that are yet to be funded, and other areas where the giver may be able to get involved. The Lord told Habakkuk to write the vision so plainly that even those who were running by could clearly see it. As the Lord speaks to a giver, it is often concerning a specific need, focus, or type of

Knowing about a need, but not driven by the need, allows the Lord to more effectively direct the giver without the noise of emotion or manipulation.

ministry. *Knowing* about a need, but *not driven* by the need, allows the Lord to more effectively direct the giver without the noise of emotion or manipulation.

Another area often overlooked is methods of giving. Most ministries are familiar only with cash giving, that is, writing a check and making a donation today. There are many other methods of giving that can help the ministry and the giver both accomplish their goals. This is one of the reasons for this book: to give ministries an understanding of some of the methods of giving that can facilitate efficient and effective giving for the giver and the ministry. The later sections of this book will provide familiarization with many of these methods and approaches and will serve as a starting point for a discussion with the giver.

Provide a Safe Haven for the Giver

As stated above, the relationship between the ministry and the giver is symbiotic. Both need the other to fulfill God's calling. God knows this. It was His idea from the beginning. The devil has tried to separate the giver from the ministry for centuries with false doctrine, greed, strife, class warfare, and anything else he could do to slow or stop the funding of the kingdom of God. Remember the part about the kingdom of God enduring violent assault? This separation of minister and giver is part of that assault.

As a result, many ministers and many givers have become isolated from each other, often mistrusting the motives of the other. The giver may think, "That ministry is just after my money; they don't care anything about me." The ministry may think, "He's just trying to control me with that donation. He's just looking to increase his power." Unfortunately, both have been true far too often, but it need not be so.

Ministries must provide a safe haven for the giver, making it clear that they are not looking to get something *from* them, but get something *to* them. Sincerity of purpose is the starting point for this safe haven. I heard a minister remark one time that they had been teaching a sermon on giving. After the sermon, someone came up to them and told them how that message had changed their whole view on giving, and as a result, they were donating a large check—*to a different ministry.* At first, the minister who gave the sermon was taken aback, but after allowing God to show them that the purpose of the sermon was to minister to the giver not get something from the giver, they became free of that hang-up and were then able to teach on giving with a free and pure heart. That is the kind of maturity that ministries need, and that maturity is required to provide a safe haven for a giver.

There are many other areas where change may be needed to unleash the gift of giving for a giver and into a ministry. Spend time and give attention to seeking the Lord on this issue so you can work with Him to unleash the gift of giving.

THE STORY (continued)
The Conference

Nathan was invited to a Christian giving conference by Gabe Miller, one of Nathan's suppliers, a very kind believer who was also quite wealthy. Nathan and Eva had been to many "giving" conferences, all of which had the same conclusion: we want you to give your money to this cause. Nathan and Eva were certainly not opposed to giving. On the contrary, they saw it as their duty given the wealth that they had. They just did not like what Nathan referred to as the "dog and pony shows" where they were only asked to give. But Gabe was insistent that this would be different, so Nathan agreed.

During the conference, Nathan and Eva were taught and challenged. They were taught what the Bible said about wealth, about giving, and about the role of the wealthy. They were taught about ways to give that were more efficient and effective than anything they had understood before. They heard testimonies from others whose lives had gone from achieving success to finding true worth since they chose to be wealthy for God. They were even taught that God was glad that they were wealthy and that it was His idea and that was how He wants to bless the people of the earth—through those who are *wealthy for God*. Nathan and Eva found themselves being challenged to give as God directed, not based on fear, manipulation, or guilt.

To be *wealthy for God* was different from anything they had ever thought of before. And most surprising of all, no one asked them to write a check at the end of the conference. The only thing they were asked to do is consider being wealthy for God in their own lives, and to talk to the conference sponsors if they wanted to learn more and pursue more efficient and effective ways to give. Nathan spoke briefly with one of the presenters and asked to be contacted so he could explore all of these new ideas further. For the first time in their lives they were excited about being rich! They wanted to know more, do more, and enjoy more, and made a decision to learn how to be wealthy for God.

Chapter 3

The Legacy

What is a Legacy?

A gift, an inheritance, something left to an heir. It sounds so simple, yet it and its implications are profound. Legacy comes from the Latin root *lego* and means to pass through. A legacy is what you pass through that will represent you when you are gone. It is so much more than tangible property; it is how to use that property. It is more than financial wealth; it is the purpose for that wealth. It carries with it the values and virtues of the one who sent it. It is how someone will be remembered after they are gone.

In his book *The Denial of Death*, Ernest Becker wrote, "This is mankind's age-old dilemma in the face of death: what man really fears is not so much extinction, but extinction with insignificance. Man wants to know that his life has somehow counted, that it has left a trace, a trace that has meaning. And in order for anything once alive to have meaning, its effects must remain alive in eternity some way." One worldwide ministry speaks to this dilemma with their purpose statement: making a mark that cannot be erased. As our society has developed with prosperity and success becoming a reality for many, the question of the reason for the pursuit of success has become nagging. Success without significance is hollow, meaningless. Success with significance is motivating, energizing, and can create a meaningful legacy.

Bob Buford, a very successful businessman, dealt with this very question and changed his pursuit from success to significance. He used his own life experiences as the foundation for his book *Halftime: Changing Your Gameplan From Success to Significance*. His analogy of halftime speaks to the point in our lives where we, like a sports team, return to the locker room to determine where we are and how we want to live the second half of our lives. How we play the first half of our lives affects the next, but it is how we finish that matters most.

The apostle Paul knew this full well. In his second letter to Timothy, a pastor and his son in the faith, Paul shares these words:

> *6For I am already being poured out as a drink offering, and the time of my departure is at hand. 7I have fought the good fight, I have finished the race, I have kept the faith. 8Finally, there is laid up for me the crown of righteousness, which the Lord, the righteous Judge, will give to me on that Day, and not to me only but also to all who have loved His appearing.*
>
> *II Timothy 4:6-8 (NKJV)*

He told his son, Timothy, that he knew his time on this earth was drawing to a close, but he made sure that Timothy knew that he had finished well. Not only was Paul concerned that Timothy know how important it was that he was finishing well, but he was also concerned that Timothy would do the same. In the prior verses, Paul exhorts Timothy:

> *¹I charge you therefore before God and the Lord Jesus Christ, who will judge the living and the dead at His appearing and His kingdom: ²Preach the word! Be ready in season and out of season. Convince, rebuke, exhort, with all longsuffering and teaching. ³For the time will come when they will not endure sound doctrine, but according to their own desires, because they have itching ears, they will heap up for themselves teachers; ⁴and they will turn their ears away from the truth, and be turned aside to fables. ⁵But you be watchful in all things, endure afflictions, do the work of an evangelist, fulfill your ministry.*
>
> *II Timothy 4:1-5 (NKJV)*

Paul knew how much Timothy had grown and matured in his calling and election, but there was still a second half awaiting him, and Paul wanted to be sure that Timothy would finish well. Timothy would be continuing in the faith he learned from his mother and grandmother, but also would be continuing Paul's legacy in the church at Ephesus.

Biblical Approach to Legacy

What does the Bible require for leaving a legacy? Is leaving a legacy really that important? What does leaving a legacy actually entail? The first part of Proverbs 13:22 is one of the most quoted scriptures surrounding inheritance. Solomon, the wisest man in the land, said that a good man leaves an inheritance to his children's children. That is not to say that he disinherits his own children for his grandchildren, but that his legacy is so significant that it will be passed down for many generations. Solomon goes on to say in Ecclesiastes 7:11 that wisdom is good with an inheritance.

Wisdom without an inheritance or an inheritance without wisdom is an easy way to not be remembered favorably! It is often easy to see how wisdom passed without wealth can fall short in accomplishing the goal in Proverbs 13:22. Jessie O'Neill, granddaughter of Charles Erwin Wilson, past president of General Motors, was born into wealth. In her book, *The Golden Ghetto: The Psychology of Affluence*, she reveals the negative effects of wealth without wisdom in what she refers to as **affluenza**, the harmful or unbalanced relationship with money or its pursuit. Author Philip Slater said in his book, *Wealth Addictions*, "Money was meant to be our servant. But when we depend on servants too much, they gradually become our masters, because we have surrendered to them our ability to run our own lives."

The Bible calls this the love of money and it is at the root of all evil. Not money, but the love of money. There are plenty of people without wealth who have the love of money, but those with money are able to leave a more devastating impact in the world. When someone couples the love of money with the money to act on that love, all sorts of manifestations of evil can result. Wisdom with an inheritance is the key to leaving a good legacy. Understanding the Biblical approach to

There are plenty of people without wealth who have the love of money, but those with money are able to leave a more devastating impact in the world.

legacy is critical to our being able to finish well and pass the right legacy to the next generations.

Everyone has an innate desire to attain and transfer meaning and significance. God put it there. It is satiated only by His plan for our lives. Even the great commission to make disciples found in Matthew 28 is a result of Jesus' building and leaving a legacy to all of mankind. He finished his commission with, "I am with you always, *even* to the end of the age." Jesus was not physically present, but His Spirit was literally with them long after His body departed. His legacy lives on today and, as He promised, will do so until the end of the age. Our part in that commission may be unique, but our requirement to leave a meaningful legacy is not.

Since the time that God told Adam to be fruitful and multiply and replenish the earth, we have had a calling and equipping to leave a legacy. God re-established that calling with Abram (Abraham) when He said:

> *¹Get out of your country,*
> *From your family*
> *And from your father's house,*
> *To a land that I will show you.*
> *²I will make you a great nation;*
> *I will bless you*
> *And make your name great;*
> *And you shall be a blessing.*
> *³I will bless those who bless you,*
> *And I will curse him who curses you;*
> *And in you all the families of the earth*
> *shall be blessed.*
> *Genesis 12:1-3 (NKJV)*

That is quite a legacy—bless all the families of the earth. As Galatians 3 tells us that we are Abraham's seed and heirs according to the promise, it is easy to see how Jesus' commission is the model legacy, and through that commission we are to bless all the families of the earth. We have a clear requirement, individually and as ministries, to build and leave a legacy that will be a blessing to the families of the earth. Even as Ephesians 5 relates that we all have different parts to play, the need for us to leave a legacy is a part of the overall legacy of Jesus Himself and should always be seen in that light. Our building and leaving a legacy is not just a good idea, it is required and has eternal significance. With that in mind, it is critical that we understand what makes up a legacy and how our legacy should be built for today and the future.

THE STORY (continued)
Reflections

After attending the conference, Nathan became more reflective about his life. He also began thinking more and more about the legacy he would leave behind when he and Eva were gone. Not just the stuff, the business and the wealth, but their children and grandchildren. With the quick success of his business, he and Eva were able to provide well for his children, giving them the best of everything, all of the things he and Eva had to do without when they were growing up.

Looking back now, it seems that Nathan spent so much time working that all his children got from him was his money, not his time, and certainly not any wisdom he accumulated over the years. Except, of course, for Chris, their oldest son who works with Nathan. Chris is Nathan's pride and joy who practically runs the company. As a result of that association, Nathan has poured all of his life lessons and his heart into Chris, who has always been responsible, focused, and receptive. Chris and his wife, Angela, and their two children, Tyler and Madison, live in the same town, go to the same church, and are nearly inseparable from Nathan and Eva. Tyler and Madison would rather be at Granddad and Mimi's house than their own.

If only he could say the same for his relationship with Jennifer, Chris' younger sister. Jennifer was certainly a good girl, a good student, and had lots of friends. With Nathan being away so much, she and Eva spent a lot of time together, and everything seemed to be going well until she went to college; that is when everything changed. She had always been a free-spirited girl, but the past fifteen years had, at best, been trying.

Now twice divorced and continually in and out of drug rehab, Jennifer is trying to raise her 14-year-old daughter Mariah. Nathan and Eva have "helped" Jennifer and Mariah throughout the years, bailing Jennifer out of one financial crisis after another. They have also had Mariah live with them several times during Jennifer's challenges. Even so, with Jennifer never wanting to have anything to do with her parents and living over 1,500 miles away, the relationship is very strained. As Nathan reflects, it occurs to him that he may not have helped Jennifer, but may have been enabling her all along.

The Capital of Legacy

Capital refers to assets, resources, investment, and wealth. It is usually measurable, used in the production of more wealth and can be transferred to another. An effective legacy consists of three facets that can be differentiated as types of capital: spiritual capital, human capital, and financial capital.

In order to build and leave an individual's or a ministry's legacy, we must understand these elements of a legacy's capital and how to properly apply them. Spiritual capital is that part which God supplies inside our spirit that He develops in us as we develop in Him. Human capital is that part which we supply that we develop through Him. Financial capital is that which God directs others to supply that we steward, use, and develop.

Spiritual capital is that part which God supplies inside our spirit that He develops in us as we develop in Him.

The Assessment: As you go through the different types of capital and their components, conduct your own inventory. Ask yourself the following:

1. Do I personally have this capital in my life? To what degree?
2. Do we need this capital in the ministry? To what degree?
3. Do we have this capital in the ministry? To what degree?
4. Do I want the ministry to pass this capital on as a legacy?

You can use the Capital Assessment located in Appendix A to record your assessment. You are free to photocopy the Capital Assessment pages to easier record your assessment. You may want to have other key people in your ministry take the assessment as well.

THE STORY (continued)
The Contact

Nathan and Eva received a phone call from Alissa Griffin, the executive director of His Story Ministries, one of the ministries that presented at the conference they attended. Nathan and Evan had spoken briefly with her at the end of the confrerence. His Story Ministries was a Christian drug and alcohol rehabilitation ministry that helped people with a history of drug and alcohol abuse trade that history for a new life in Christ, with His Story being their new history, based on II Corinthians 5:17: "Therefore, if anyone is in Christ, he is a new creation; old things have passed away; behold, all things have become new." When Alissa shared the His Story approach, Nathan and Eva thought about their daughter, Jennifer, and how much they wished His Story could help her.

Nathan and Eva met with Alissa for lunch later that week. They shared with her about their experience at the conference, how much they learned, and how much they wanted to live a life of true worth and leave a meaningful legacy. They also shared how they wanted to help Jennifer and that they wanted to explore ways of helping the vision of His Story Ministries. Alissa recommended they meet with Luke Edwards, the Christian legacy advisor who

---

spoke at the conference. She explained how he had helped other couples and individuals who had a similar desire to leave a meaningful legacy and that he could also help them work through the delicate issues surrounding their desire to help Jennifer. After lunch, Nathan and Eva called Luke Edwards and set up a time to meet.

Spiritual Capital

Spiritual capital is given to us as an internal gift from God. This capital is uniquely designed to equip us to accomplish our role in His kingdom. This spiritual capital includes vision, integrity, mandates, ministry gifting, and functional gifting. These elements together make up the measure of spiritual capital in a legacy.

Vision

Vision includes the end result of your spiritual reason for existence. A familiar scripture relating to vision is Habakkuk 2:2-4:

> *Then the LORD answered me and said: "Write the vision and make it plain on tablets, that he may run who reads it. For the vision is yet for an appointed time; But at the end it will speak, and it will not lie. Though it tarries, wait for it; because it will surely come, it will not tarry. Behold the proud, His soul is not upright in him; But the just shall live by his faith" (NKJV).*

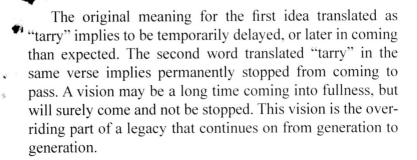

The original meaning for the first idea translated as "tarry" implies to be temporarily delayed, or later in coming than expected. The second word translated "tarry" in the same verse implies permanently stopped from coming to pass. A vision may be a long time coming into fullness, but will surely come and not be stopped. This vision is the overriding part of a legacy that continues on from generation to generation.

Integrity

The idea of integrity is critical to a legacy. David said in Psalm 41:12, *"As for me, You uphold me in my integrity, and set me before Your face forever" (NKJV).* That is a critical element of establishing and leaving a legacy. Solomon exhorts in Proverbs 11:3: *"The integrity of the upright will guide them, but the perversity of the unfaithful will destroy them" (NKJV).*

Integrity is being true to your vision, your calling, your God, and

The presence or absence of integrity does not determine whether or not one will leave a legacy; it governs the type of legacy one will surely leave behind.

your word. It is doing what is right when no one is looking. It is maintaining moral courage above pressure. It is being all that God says you can and should be and refusing to be anything less. The presence or absence of integrity does not determine whether or not one will leave a legacy; it governs the quality of legacy one will surely leave behind.

Mandates

There are good ideas, there are suggestions, and then there are those tasks that God has assigned to you and your ministry that, without accomplishing these tasks, the vision will not come to pass for you and possibly pass to another. These are mandates. Mandate comes from the Latin *mandare* meaning to entrust, enjoin, and is akin to *manus* (hand) and *dere* (to put). Jesus was more than a little clear when dealing with mandates.

> [57]*Now it happened as they journeyed on the road, that someone said to Him, "Lord, I will follow You wherever You go." [58]And Jesus said to him, "Foxes have holes and birds of the air have nests, but the Son of Man has nowhere to lay His head." [59]Then He said to another, "Follow Me."*
>
> *But he said, "Lord, let me first go and bury my father." [60]Jesus said to him, "Let the dead bury their own dead, but you go and preach the kingdom of God." [61]And another also said, "Lord, I will follow You, but let me first go and bid them farewell who are at my house." [62]But Jesus said to him, "No one, having put his hand to the plow, and looking back, is fit for the kingdom of God." [1]After these things the Lord appointed seventy others also, and sent them two by two before His face into every city and place where He Himself was about to go. [2]Then He said to them, "The harvest truly is great, but the laborers are few; therefore pray the Lord of*

> *the harvest to send out laborers into His har-*
> *vest. ³Go your way; behold, I send you out as*
> *lambs among wolves.*
>
> Luke 9:57-10:3 (NKJV)

Jesus did not mince words about putting your hand to your work, or completing a mandate. In verse 62 above, those who would not respond properly to His mandate were not fit for the kingdom of God. What does that say about our attitude of trying something until we grow tired of it? Paul encourages the Galatians with, *"And let us not grow weary while doing good, for in due season we shall reap if we do not lose heart" (Gal 6:9 NKJV).* The spiritual capital of knowing and accomplishing God's mandates is essential in establishing and leaving a legacy.

Ministry Gifting

> *¹¹And He Himself gave some to be apos-*
> *tles, some prophets, some evangelists, and*
> *some pastors and teachers, ¹²for the equip-*
> *ping of the saints for the work of ministry,*
> *for the edifying of the body of Christ, ¹³till*
> *we all come to the unity of the faith and of*
> *the knowledge of the Son of God, to a perfect*
> *man, to the measure of the stature of the full-*
> *ness of Christ; ¹⁴that we should no longer be*
> *children, tossed to and fro and carried about*
> *with every wind of doctrine, by the trickery*
> *of men, in the cunning craftiness of deceitful*
> *plotting, ¹⁵but, speaking the truth in love,*
> *may grow up in all things into Him who is the*
> *head—Christ— ¹⁶from whom the whole body,*

*joined and knit together by what every joint
supplies, according to the effective working
by which every part does its share, causes
growth of the body for the edifying of itself
in love.*

Ephesians 4:11-16 (NKJV)

Ministry gifting is often referred to as your calling. Some are called to be pastors; some are called to be evangelists. Some have multiple callings on their life and those callings work together to bring about the vision that God has called them to fulfill. These giftings are often referred to as the five-fold ministry gifts and are the gifts that God Himself gives to equip the body of Christ to do the work of the ministry. The equipping is, as stated in verses 14 and 15, to help the body of Christ grow up into maturity to properly perform the work of the ministry. Just as a child needs certain elements for growth and maturity, so does the body of Christ in order to reach maturity. A child does not, nor should not be expected to, have the capacity to do the work of a fully-mature adult. The apostle, prophet, evangelist, pastor, and teacher are used to mature the body of Christ to complete their work on the earth.

Apostle

The gift of apostle enables one to provide leadership and accountability over a number of pastors and churches. The apostle, one sent forth, is often the one who begins and oversees new ministries or churches, providing spiritual and strategic leadership to those organizations as they fulfill their missions in the kingdom of God.

Prophet

The gift of the prophet is the white blood cell of the body of Christ: one who attacks contamination and infections that would damage the body. This is not to be confused with self-appointed judges who criticize other ministries that they neither understand nor accept. Called to minister to those inside the body of Christ, the true prophet deals with contamination from within: sin. Often through strong scripture-based preaching, the prophet calls members of the body of Christ to higher levels of holiness and communion with God the Father with an exhortation to repent of areas that have held them back from maturity.

Evangelist

The evangelist is the most well-known gift outside of the pastor. Called to minister to those outside the body of Christ, this gift equips the believer to actively initiate and develop a relationship with unbelievers in order to share the Gospel of Jesus Christ effectively and easily, bringing many into a personal relationship with Jesus as their Lord and Savior and beginning them on their journey with the Lord.

Pastor

The gift of pastor assumes responsibility for the growth, maturity, and development of a group of believers. Called to minister to those inside the body of Christ, specifically in their congregation, the pastor guards the body from outside predators by instilling in them the pure milk of the Word (1 Peter 2:2) and the solid food of the word of righteousness (Hebrews 5:13-14) to keep them built up and strong. The pastor provides direction, teaching, loving, accountability, and correction, and provides an example to help the members of the group become spiritually mature and effective members of the kingdom of God.

Teacher

The gift of teacher is the ability to take complex topics and information and convey them to others in a clear and practical manner. Those with the gift of teaching are the ones who, once they understand a Biblical truth, can teach it to others with passion and practicality, helping the learner grow in their walk with God and their understanding of His kingdom.

Functional Gifting

Outside of the ministry giftings above, those giftings that make up the work of the ministry can be referred to as functional gifting. Your functional gifting can also be referred to as your part of the great commission or your job description. In the book of Romans, Paul shares:

> *⁴For as we have many members in one body, but all the members do not have the same function, ⁵so we, being many, are one body in Christ, and individually members of one another. ⁶Having then gifts differing according to the grace that is given to us, let us use them: if prophecy, let us prophesy in proportion to our faith; ⁷or ministry, let us use it in our ministering; he who teaches, in teaching; ⁸he who exhorts, in exhortation; he who gives, with liberality; he who leads, with diligence; he who shows mercy, with cheerfulness.*
>
> *Romans 12:4-8 (NKJV)*

For example, you may be called to be an evangelist to the nations. You may be called to start a company that designs and builds specialty trucks for use by evangelists that are called to the nations. You may be called to purchase and give those trucks to evangelists that are called to the nations. You may be called to drive one of those trucks for an evangelist that is called to the nations. All of these functional callings are necessary parts of evangelism, but not all the functions are the same. They, along with many others, represent different functions required to work together to accomplish the calling of an evangelist. This concept is outlined in Ephesians 4:16: *"from whom the whole body, joined and knit together by what every joint supplies, according to the effective working by which every part does its share, causes growth of the body for the edifying of itself in love" (NKJV).* Everyone is working together doing their part that is effective, the part which they are especially good at doing and like to do.

Too many times, well-meaning Christians work in an area of ministry that they neither enjoy nor have any competence in, yet they wonder why they "burn out" or are not satisfied in their "service" to the Lord. According to Ephesians 4:16, there is a part that is effective for them. It's finding that gifting and a place to use it that causes most of the problem.

Too many times, well-meaning Christians work in an area of ministry that they are neither competent nor enjoy, yet they wonder why they "burn out" or are not satisfied in their "service" to the Lord.

How ridiculous would it be to expect an evangelist who is called to the nations to design and build a truck, personally pay for the truck, and then drive the truck just to get to do the evangelist tasks that he's called to do? After he spent the time and money to become trained in special truck design, learned how to build the special trucks, and then got his special truck driving license, there would not be very much money, time, or energy left to pay for the truck, let alone drive it. And then there is no time, money, energy, or anointing left to go to the nations to evangelize. Too many in ministry are trying to do all the functional giftings needed to accomplish their calling. No wonder so many people entering into full-time ministry quit! And what is worse is that they are leaving a trail of gifted but frustrated truck design engineers, truck builders, truck drivers, and truck givers with no place to use their gifting. By operating outside their own ministry and functional gifting, they are denying others the ability to use their giftings for ministry.

Often those same gifted and frustrated folks have never been taught that what they are really good at and really like to do is what God has called them to do for the kingdom of God. There's been such a separation between "ministry" and secular vocations that the whole idea of being called to the ministry of truck design or truck driving has been completely overlooked. The gift of giving is certainly not the only gift that needs to be unleashed. It is way past time to get that major misconception cleared up in the body of Christ!

The verses in Romans 12 mentioned above give us a sample of some of the functional giftings that are needed in the body of Christ. Below is a list of some of the more common delineations of functional giftings that are available to assist those in the five-fold ministry gifts in the work of the ministry:

Missionary

The gift of the missionary is the ability to minister in cultures other than your own. This missionary can operate as an apostle, prophet, evangelist, pastor, teacher, doctor, or truck driver, but does so in a different country or culture. These are the ones who work on the front lines of the great commission, taking the kingdom of God into the world.

Helps

Helps is the gifting that helps get things done. They enable other Christians to be effective and fruitful in ministry by doing practical and necessary tasks. Whether an usher in a worship service, an audio-visual technician that perfects the sound and video system, or one who personally assists a member of the five-fold ministry gifts, they are the ones who work behind the scenes to allow ministry to occur.

Leadership

The gift of leadership is the ability to guide and mentor others in following a vision that is part of advancing the kingdom of God. The gift of leadership is part of a legacy's spiritual capital; leadership executed is part of a legacy's human capital and is discussed further in that section. One who has the gift of leadership can make a seemingly complex and insurmountable goal seem attainable and is able to interject motivation, hope, and zeal in the followers while equipping those followers to grow in their own leadership abilities.

Administration

The gift of administration is the ability to organize and coordinate information, people, and projects. As opposed to leadership, the gift of administration deals more with managing, planning, and maintaining than creating followership. Working with the vision of the leader, this gifting makes sure the plans and projects needed to bring the vision to pass are on track smoothly and efficiently while equipping the followers with the practical steps needed to follow the leader.

Craftsmanship

Craftsmanship is the ability to work with your hands to build, design, or create things that benefit other believers. In Exodus 31, Moses appointed people filled with the Spirit of God in wisdom and understanding of craftsmanship to create the items of the tabernacle, working with gold, brass, wood, tapestry, and construction. The gift of craftsmanship enhances the physical surroundings to make them functional and attractive and to bring glory to God.

Service

The gift of service is the desire to help others with a need, be it a task or calling. The gift of service can be expressed in something as simple as helping a single mother by offering to babysit and clean her house while she takes some time for herself. This gift is like the oil in the engine—without it, many of the moving parts would grind to a halt, become damaged, and no longer be effective. We are all called to serve one another at a certain level; those with this gift make it look easy.

Giving

The gift of giving is the ability to generously and cheerfully contribute wealth to the kingdom of God. Those with the gift of giving often discover financial needs and provide for those needs out of their abundance, operating as an extension of Jehovah Jireh, the one who sees and provides. This gift will be covered in much more detail in other sections of this book.

Music

The gift of music is the ability to contribute to a worship experience through voice or instrument. This gift is used to bring glory and praise to God and help usher others into the presence of God through praise and worship.

Knowledge

The gift of knowledge is the ability to research, study, and organize facts and information on different subjects. This gift, working with the gift of teaching, allows these newly discovered or re-discovered truths to be passed on to help the body of Christ mature and develop.

Wisdom

The gift of wisdom discerns the mind of Christ. This enables the believer to understand and apply scriptural truths to specific situations, helping others to make Godly choices and decisions.

Prayer

The gift of prayer is the ability to pray for significant lengths of time in all types of prayer as directed by the Spirit of God. People with this gift pray fervently for the needs of the body of Christ and the needs of the kingdom of God. According to James 5:16, these often unseen warriors in the Spirit make "tremendous power available, dynamic in its working" (Amplified), thus empowering the other gifts to operate in higher levels of effectiveness.

Hospitality

The gift of hospitality is the ability to make someone feel at home, welcome, loved, and cared for as a part of a group. This is the "pound cake and coffee" gift—an open heart, a listening ear, an acceptance without judgment. This gift helps create an atmosphere that encourages people to be at ease and feel loved and valued as they grow in maturity.

Mercy

The gift of mercy is the ability to feel sincere compassion and brings practical relief and hope to people who are hurting. People with the gift of mercy do not feel sympathy for people, but empathy, relating to their need, pain, or problem. Jesus was moved by compassion wherever He went, meeting the needs of all who would accept His gift. Those with this gift help bring practical relief for the hurts and pains, helping the one in pain to grow and mature in their walk with the Lord and in their place in the kingdom of God.

Exhortation

The gift of exhortation is the coach of the body of Christ—the coach helps the good get better, sometimes with encouragement, sometimes with a rebuke. Lovingly holding someone accountable, the exhorter is always helping the one being exhorted to excel and grow in their position in the Kingdom of God.

When we all recognize and work in our functional giftings, either in a five-fold ministry gift position or as a minister who works outside those ministry gifts to bring their supply to support the body of Christ, we will be that mature body of Christ with each part doing, and loving, their part.

We can joyfully work in our giftings with integrity, accomplishing our mandates to bring to pass the vision God has placed on the inside of us. In other words, we can maximize our spiritual capital.

THE STORY (continued)
The Process

Nathan and Eva were not sure what to expect in their meeting with Luke Edwards. During the conference, he had explained many ways to give that were more efficient and effective than anything they had understood before. The stories he told sounded so wonderful, but they wondered if their situation could have such a happy ending.

Luke shared some of his background, some of how he helps families design plans to leave meaningful legacies tomorrow while still accomplishing their financial goals today. But most of all, Luke asked questions—lots of questions. He asked them questions that no one had ever asked—questions regarding their family, their dreams, their concerns, and their goals.

After nearly two hours, Nathan and Eva began to realize how little thinking and planning they had done for their future. They asked Luke what they should do next to help develop their plans for their meaningful legacy. Luke laid out a multi-step process that began with a legacy vision retreat, a time where Luke would meet with them and help them discover their true vision for their family's legacy. This legacy vision retreat would also crystallize their vision into a family legacy vision statement, a concise summary of how they had become wealthy, their

---

vision and priorities for their wealth, and their vision for leaving a meaningful legacy for future generations. This summary would provide the basis for all of the other decisions related to designing their family legacy plan.

Nathan and Eva scheduled the weekend retreat with Luke and decided to hold the retreat at their mountain cabin where they could work uninterrupted by phone calls and other distractions. Luke gave them each a book with questions to work on before the retreat, and he told them to work independently and that they would go over the questions during the retreat. As Nathan and Eva left Luke's office, they finally had a peace that they were going in the right direction.

Human Capital

Human capital is that part which we supply that we develop through Him. This human capital includes leadership, intellectual capacity, physical capacity, spiritual capacity, and organizational capacity. There is little written or taught on human capital from a kingdom of God perspective, but understanding and properly developing our human capital is critical in the kingdom of God.

Leadership

President Dwight D. Eisenhower stated, "Leadership is the art of getting someone else to do something you want done because he wants to do it." Greatness in leadership is the ability to cast a vision that others want to follow and the mentoring of those followers, developing them in their ability to subsequently lead others. It is not the ability to manipulate and coerce people into following the dictates of a tyrannical egocentric. This antithesis of good leadership is best seen in a quote by a dynamic, yet duplicitous, leader, Adolf Hitler: "What luck for rulers that men do not think." In order for a leader to lead in greatness, the followers must not only think, but think creatively to assist the leader in accomplishing the vision. Without that, you are not leading in greatness. Leadership expert, author, and speaker John Maxwell says, "He who thinks he leads, but has no followers, is only taking a walk."

Effective leaders direct followers to generate productive change to achieve desired goals or objectives, never taking their eye off the vision. The most clear and compelling mission statements with the best designed plans become mere academic exercises without good leadership. Leadership is not merely the ability to make an initial decision on a goal; it is the consistently executed ability to make ongoing decisions during the implementation of those compelling mission statements and well-designed plans, especially in the face of unexpected changes to the environment, the participants, and realized errors in the assumptions made during the planning process.

Leadership is also about serving. Some of the most successful leaders in ministry and industry were servant leaders

Leadership is also about serving. Some of the most successful leaders in ministry and industry were servant leaders who served God and their followers with their heart and their resources.

who served God and their followers with their heart and their resources.

Case Study: Godly Leadership Yields Results

In 1897, Jim, a young store clerk raised on a farm in Missouri, moved west for health reasons. At 24 years old, Jim began work as an entry-level clerk for a dry goods store in Wyoming. Within two years, the company offered to make him a partner in a new store in the mining town of Kemmerer, Wyoming. Using his life savings and borrowing the rest, he became a one-third partner in the new store he called the "Golden Rule." Raised in a Christian home with the utmost respect for the Lord and honest business, his idea was "to make money and build business through serving the community with fair and honest value."

His hard work and persistence yielded great success. Within five years, he bought out his partners and began two additional stores in other towns. His success included treating his employees well and developing leaders. As his store managers became successful and saved enough money, Jim would help them start their own store as one-third owner as long as the manager would train someone to take his place at the existing store. Jim would put up the other two-thirds needed to start the new store. This new owner/leader would, in turn, train other managers, making them ready to start their own stores as one-third owners.

After just two years, in 1909, Jim left the original store and went to Salt Lake City to establish a headquarters for the growing chain. Within three years, Jim had grown the chain to 28 stores in six states. After incorporating in 1913, Jim moved the headquarters to New York City to be closer to his major suppliers. Between 1920 and 1930, the new company opened more than 1,250 new stores on Main Streets in small towns all through America, including through the Great Depression. Jim, an ardent tither, went from giving the first 10% of his income to the work of the Lord to giving away 90% of his income. With the blessing of God on his life, Jim served as chairman of the board of the company until 1958 and as a director until his death in 1971. James Cash Penney is an example of greatness in servant leadership with a legacy of good merchandise at a fair and honest value still alive in JC Penney stores today.

Leadership is fluid. Leadership is deliberate. Leadership is decisive. Leadership is vision-oriented and people-focused. Leadership is an indispensable part of human capital needed to build a meaningful and lasting legacy.

Intellectual Capacity

Our intellectual capacity is the part of human capital that connects our vision and calling with the execution of our vision and calling through research, ideas, and plans. Intellectual capacity includes all of our acquired knowledge, wisdom, and understanding, as well as our potential for increasing in knowledge, wisdom, and understanding. It is applying the knowledge, wisdom, and understanding that generates the plans which guide the accomplishment of our vision and mandates. Although we can do nothing to change the present amount of knowledge, wisdom, and understanding amassed, our choices today and going forward certainly affect our potential and future levels.

Learning

One of the keys to increasing our intellectual capacity is learning. Although that may sound simplistic, I am not referring to what we learn alone, but the very process of learning itself increases our capacity to learn more. Something as simple as increasing our vocabulary actually increases our ability to conceptualize and retain new information as well as think creatively. The greatest leaders of successful ministries and industries are well-known learners. Author and speaker Michael Pink recently led devotions at the Ziglar Corporation. Zig Ziglar, the infamous speaker, writer, motivator, and sales expert, who is in his early eighties, attended. Not only did he attend, but took notes and asked questions. He later told Michael Pink that he not only reads his Bible and the newspaper every day, he also spends an average of four hours a day reading materials to help him grow. When we stop learning, we do not just stop growing; we begin the process of mental atrophy, the slow wasting away of our intellectual capacity.

Renewing

Another key to increasing our intellectual capacity is doing what the Bible refers to as renewing our mind.

> *[1]I beseech you therefore, brethren, by the mercies of God, that you present your bodies a living sacrifice, holy, acceptable to God, which is your reasonable service. [2]And do not be conformed to this world, but be transformed by the renewing of your mind, that you may prove what is that good and acceptable and perfect will of God.*
>
> *Romans 12:1-2 (NKJV)*

So what does it actually mean to renew our minds? The word "renew" comes from the Greek word *anakainosis*, which means renewal, renovation, complete change for the better. Webster's 1828 dictionary defines renew as "to make new; to renovate; to transform; to change from natural enmity to the love of God and his law; to implant holy affections in the heart; to regenerate." Renew means more than just a coat of paint and a new couch. When you renovate a house, you do not just add new furnishings and fixtures. You completely remove any trace of the old that is no longer beneficial. You may tear out everything, including the proverbial kitchen sink. You may even rearrange walls, rooms, or add on new rooms. The goal is to make the home into a completely new environment.

Our minds can become so full of the "wisdom" of the world that it creates a paradigm, not just a set of facts, but a whole viewpoint in which new information is viewed. If we have a flawed world view, we will never see situations in the proper perspective. What perspective should we have? The Bible is very clear on that point. I Corinthians 2:16 says that we are not able to instruct the Lord, "but we have the mind of Christ."

The Amplified Bible goes on to say in verse 16, "But we have the mind of Christ (the Messiah) and do hold the thoughts (feelings and purposes) of His heart. Not only do we have the mind (thoughts and perspective) of Christ, but even the thoughts, feelings and purposes of His heart.

So how do we replace, renovate, and transform our minds? First, we must decide that God's perspective is right. Anything else is inferior. Three of the four Gospel accounts record Jesus explaining the greatest commandments.

> [37]*Jesus said to him, " 'You shall love the LORD your God with all your heart, with all your soul, and with all your mind.' *[38]*This is the first and great commandment. *[39]*And the second is like it: 'You shall love your neighbor as yourself.' *[40]*On these two commandments hang all the Law and the Prophets."*
>
> *Matthew 27:37-40 (NKJV)*

We cannot truly say that we love the Lord if we do not love Him with our mind. This is so important that Jesus even says in verse 40 that all of the Law and Prophets hang on these first two commandments. All of our covenant and our future are hanging on our loving God with our heart, soul, and mind. After we make the firm decision to yield our thoughts and preconceived ideas to His thoughts, we can proceed to renovate our mind.

The second step is to actively find out the mind of God. Many people believe it is impossible to know what God is thinking. Even though I Corinthians 2:16 (above) clearly says we do, many people are trapped with experiential knowledge instead of revelation knowledge. They only believe what they have experienced themselves. Many well-meaning Christians and theologians go to great lengths to explain why we cannot have what God says we already have, just because they are not currently experiencing it. I call this experiential theology—"I experience, therefore it must be."

What arrogance to think that the word of God does not work just because someone has not experienced it working.

What arrogance to think that the word of God does not work just because someone has not experienced it working. That is borderline humanism. Often quoting portions of scripture to support their flawed paradigm, one would think that God wants to keep us in the dark and never let us know His will. One often-quoted passage used to illustrate an inability to understand God is found in I Corinthians 2:

> *⁶However, we speak wisdom among those who are mature, yet not the wisdom of this age, nor of the rulers of this age, who are coming to nothing. ⁷But we speak the wisdom of God in a mystery, the hidden wisdom which God ordained before the ages for our glory, ⁸which none of the rulers of this age knew; for had they known, they would not have crucified the Lord of glory. ⁹But as it is written:*
> *"Eye has not seen, nor ear heard,*
> *Nor have entered into the heart of man*
> *The things which God has prepared for those who love Him" (NKJV).*

If we stop there, it seems hopeless to ever understand God. This passage has been misused to validate those who do not understand the ways of God. It was even misquoted by a national political figure in 1992:

> *We can seize this moment, make it exciting and energizing and heroic to be American again. We can renew our faith in each other and in ourselves. We can restore our sense of unity and community.*

> *As the Scripture says, "our eyes have not yet seen, nor our ears heard, nor our minds imagined" what we can build.*
>
> *But I can't do this alone—no [leader] can. We must do it together. It won't be easy and it won't be quick. We didn't get into this mess overnight, and we won't get out of it overnight. But we can do it—with commitment, creativity, diversity, and drive!*
>
> *We can do it!*
>
> *We can do it! We can do it! We can do it! We can do it! We can do it! We can do it!*

This political figure (no, I will not name him) even went as far as to take an inability to understand God's ways and turn it into blatant humanism—we can do it ourselves if we just work together. Neither approach is true. It may be something experienced, but the Bible is clear if we just keep reading the next three verses!

> [10]*But God has revealed them to us through His Spirit. For the Spirit searches all things, yes, the deep things of God.* [11]*For what man knows the things of a man except the spirit of the man which is in him? Even so no one knows the things of God except the Spirit of God.* [12]*Now we have received, not the spirit of the world, but the Spirit who is from God, that we might know the things that have been freely given to us by God (NKJV).*

This is the key: God reveals His wisdom to us through His Spirit to our Spirit, which we can then comprehend in our renewed mind, *that we might know* the things God had given to us freely. This comes from the same chapter as verse 16 above that says we have the mind of Christ!

If anyone is still in doubt that God wants us to know about Him and His wisdom, just look in the first chapter of James.

> *[5]If any of you lacks wisdom, let him ask of God, who gives to all liberally and without reproach, and it will be given to him. [6]But let him ask in faith, with no doubting, for he who doubts is like a wave of the sea driven and tossed by the wind. [7]For let not that man suppose that he will receive anything from the Lord; [8]he is a double-minded man, unstable in all his ways.*
>
> *James 1:5-8 (NKJV)*

God gives wisdom! He gives it without reproach. God does not get mad because we lack wisdom. He wants us to come to him. Just like all the promises in the Bible, there is a condition: ask in faith. What faith? Faith that He will provide the wisdom as He has promised. Without that faith, we are unstable and should not expect to receive anything from the Lord.

So the first step is to decide to submit to God's wisdom. The second step is to actively find out His wisdom. The third step is to do it! Do what God says do. It is so simple, yet so profound, and so profoundly missed by so many. Many people are so worried about how things will turn out if they really do what God says do. That is nothing new. Jesus dealt with that with the first miracle—the wedding feast at Cana.

As the story goes, they ran out of wine at the wedding feast. In John 2:5, Mary told the servants, "Whatever He says to you, do it." How simple. Just do what He says do. But what did He say? Fill water pots with water, then take the contents of the pot to the master of the feast. I can only imagine the trepidation of a servant potentially taking a goblet of water to the master of the feast when it was supposed to be wine. The Bible only tells "And He said to them 'Draw some out now, and take it to the master of the feast.' And they took it." How simple. He said; they did. And, they were not embarrassed.

As James 1:6 exhorts us to ask for wisdom in faith, the implication is not only to ask trusting that you will hear, but also trusting that you will do what you hear. James goes on to say in Chapter 2 verse 20 that faith without works is dead, or that faith without corresponding action is ineffective and worthless. Our most obvious action of faith is to do what God says to do.

As we continue to learn, we increase our knowledge and our capacity to learn more. In renewing our mind—deciding to submit to God's wisdom, seeking and hearing His wisdom, and then acting on His wisdom—we allow Him to do mighty things in our lives. Like the servants at the wedding feast, we will not be embarrassed, but will see amazing results. We will grow in knowledge, wisdom, and understanding as well as grow our potential for increasing in knowledge, wisdom, and understanding, thereby maximizing our intellectual capacity.

Physical Capacity

> *[19]Or do you not know that your body is the temple of the Holy Spirit who is in you,*

> *whom you have from God, and you are not your own? [20]For you were bought at a price; therefore glorify God in your body and in your spirit, which are God's.*
>
> *I Corinthians 6:19-20 (NKJV)*

Our physical capacity is the part of human capital that allows us to live, to be active, and to physically accomplish all that God has called us to do. We cannot be doers of the Word in fullness if we are not physically able to get out of bed or walk around the block. I am not referring to a physical disability as a result of an injury or illness, although that certainly impedes our ability to come and go as we please. I am referring to our physical fitness. Yes, this is a book on building and leaving a ministry legacy, but there are too many ministers leaving that legacy early due to low physical capacity. To be blunt, they die before they should because they did not develop physical fitness. Their ability to build a legacy for the next generation is stopped short by a heart attack, stroke, or other complication due to bad health habits. We need to quickly dispense with the idea that it is really up to us whether or not we choose to follow God's guidelines for our body. Verse 19 above tells us rather sternly that we are not our own—we have been purchased! Making sure we do what is necessary to ensure good health is a critical part of our human capital. Without it, the rest of human capital is impaired or lost.

We need to quickly dispense with the idea that it is really up to us whether or not we choose to follow God's guidelines for our body.

Dr. Don Colbert, a Christian physician who specializes in healthy living, has written the *New York Times* best selling book, *The Seven Pillars of Health,* an outstanding guide to health and nutrition. This book covers all of the sections below and more and includes an easy-to-follow plan for incorporating the Seven Pillars of Health. I highly recommend this valuable resource for building and maintaining your physical capacity.

Exercise.

Paul said in I Timothy 4:8 that exercise profits a little. So many people have used that verse as rationalization for lack of exercise. So are we to assume that a God who, according to III John 2, desires that we prosper and are in good health above all things, does not want us to exercise and it does not profit anything? How silly. The actual Greek in verse 8 says that physical training is advantageous for a short duration. Without continued physical training, any physical benefit derived is lost if the training is not maintained. In other words, you cannot lift weights once a year and expect anything but muscle cramps! It takes disciplined and consistent training to build and maintain the benefits. The benefits of exercise include increased strength and stamina, lower heart

When we take the steps necessary to maintain our health, we have a greater physical capacity to build a legacy, both in time and effectiveness. If we do not, our legacy may transfer to the next generation like a premature baby: weak, dependent, and before its time.

rate and blood pressure, stress management, and longevity. Without it, you cannot expect to maximize a full daily workload, let alone a legacy.

Proper Nutrition

With the advent of so much information on health and nutrition, everyone is without excuse. Much research and information is available in books, on the internet, on audio and video, in support groups, and from well-respected Christian physicians who practice what they preach. I will not attempt to summarize any of the specific information, but suffice it to say that a low-fat high-fiber healthy diet of grains, fruits, vegetables, and dairy products coupled with plenty of water will be much better for your body than a diet of hot dogs, fries, and soda.

When we take the steps necessary to maintain our health, we have a greater physical capacity to build a legacy, both in time and effectiveness. If we do not, our legacy may transfer to the next generation like a premature baby: weak, dependent, and before its time. It is very important to us, to God, and to the next generation.

Spiritual Capacity

Our spiritual capacity is the part of human capital that hears, processes, and acts in faith on the plans and ways of God. It is the part attributed to being able to live a Godly life, be led by the Spirit, and accomplish things in the kingdom of God.

Someone in ministry may think that they, almost by osmosis or by default, are growing spiritually because of all they are doing for God and for God's people. That does not make any more sense than saying that someone is a master mechanic just because they spend lots of time driving a car. We are each, first and foremost, individual children of the most high God and must relate to Him individually. To grow spiritually requires time spent in fellowship with God through prayer and praise and worship, time spent in fellowship with God's word through study and meditation, and time spent in fellowship with God's family in corporate worship and study as well as personal interaction.

When we become too busy in the service of God to spend time growing in our relationship with God, we are too busy, and our "service" may not be His service at all. How can we know if we are properly serving someone we do not even know? If we "minister" to others out of our own spiritual supply, not out of the overflow, we are committing treachery against our own spirit. This process cannot be sustained and will result in becoming spiritually weak and ineffective.

After we have spent quality time in His presence through praise and worship and prayer, in His word and with His body, we need to be sure to exercise our spirit by acting in faith on what his word tells us to do, both in the written word and the word spoken into our hearts. It is this process of hearing and doing that builds confidence in the kingdom of God. Staying steadfast and seeing success from obeying God builds our faith and expectation for the next challenge. Acting on what God tells us to do also qualifies us for higher levels of spiritual responsibility in the kingdom of God as illustrated in the parable of the talents mentioned earlier.

Out of all the other areas of capacity, building our spiritual capacity has an overriding positive impact on all the other areas in our life. It also has the greatest impact in the kingdom of God as we mature in our position and giftings, increasing our capacity to build and leave a Godly legacy.

Organizational Capacity

Our organizational capacity is not our ability to keep our closet neat. It is our ability to interrelate within an organization, specifically other members of the body of Christ. This involves how we handle working together in our functional gifts, relating to God's authority, and handling conflicts that arise. Much has been written and studied and taught about secular organizational behavior and performance, but it seems that very little is known about how the organization, or organism, of the body of Christ should be working together to increase efficiency, decrease injury and disease, and gain strength and maturity.

Leadership

Although leadership has already been dealt with earlier, it is important to understand the role of leadership in setting the tone for the organization. The leader is charged with leading the organization to bring to pass the vision of the organization. In order for the organization to develop and mature, the leader must set the tone and direction of the organizational climate, thereby creating an organizational environment that best accomplishes the mandates required to fulfill the vision.

It seems that very little is known about how the organization, or organism, of the body of Christ should be working together to increase efficiency, decrease injury and disease, and gain strength and maturity.

Paul charges Timothy with these words:

> *[1]You therefore, my son, be strong in the grace that is in Christ Jesus. [2]And the things that you have heard from me among many witnesses, commit these to faithful men who will be able to teach others also.*
>
> *II Timothy 2:1-2 (NKJV)*

It is not sufficient to teach an organization merely the skills to complete a given task. You must teach them also how to develop in leadership to take on increasing levels of responsibility, thereby increasing the effectiveness of the organization. Part of that development is how the members of an organization should conduct themselves in interactions with peers, leaders, and subordinates. Without continually reinforcing the right organizational behaviors, strife and enmity can quickly creep in and cripple or destroy the organization from within.

> *[13]Who is wise and understanding among you? Let him show by good conduct that his works are done in the meekness of wisdom. [14]But if you have bitter envy and self-seeking in your hearts, do not boast and lie against the truth. [15]This wisdom does not descend from above, but is earthly, sensual, demonic. [16]For where envy and self-seeking exist, confusion and every evil thing are there. [17]But the wisdom that is from above is first pure, then peaceable, gentle, willing to yield, full of mercy and good fruits, without partiality and without hypoc-*

> risy. [18]Now the fruit of righteousness is sown
> in peace by those who make peace.
>
> James 3:13-18 (NKJV)

Notice how James lists envy and self-seeking with earthly, sensual, and demonic? Not only that, but when self-seeking exists, it is accompanied by confusion and every evil thing. That is not what an organization needs! Compare that with God's way for an organization: pure, peaceable, gentle, willing to yield, full of mercy, no hypocrisy.

As a leader, you must set a clear organizational behavior standard—and live that standard yourself. You must enforce that standard within the organization. I realize enforce sounds like a strong word to use for a ministry, especially since many of the members of the organization may be volunteer workers. Well, mandate is a strong word also, and mandates are from God Himself. If someone in an organization is self-seeking, how much productivity are they adding? How much loss of productivity are they causing in others? There are two basic choices for this individual— either *they* renew their mind or *you* replace them. Either way, you cannot allow this bad behavior to continue. If faced

If faced with the choice between enforcing Godly behavior in an organization and failing to accomplish His mandates, the choice should be clear.

with the choice between enforcing Godly behavior in an organization and failing to accomplish His mandates, the choice should be clear. Furthermore, remember that enforcing behavior free of envy and self-seeking yields a pure and peaceable organizational environment for those who are not self-seeking productive members.

This is not an inconsequential matter. If you, the leader of a ministry, do not train your organization in these areas, you may soon be without an organization—and that would be a tragedy. It is that serious and it is a critical part of building and leaving a Godly legacy.

Walking in Love

> [8]*Above all things* *have intense and unfailing love for one another, for love covers a multitude of sins [forgives and disregards the offenses of others].* [9]*Practice hospitality to one another (those of the household of faith). [Be hospitable, be a lover of strangers, with brotherly affection for the unknown guests, the foreigners, the poor, and all others who come your way who are of Christ's body.] And [in each instance] do it ungrudgingly (cordially and graciously, without complaining but as representing Him).*
>
> *I Peter 4:8-9 (Amplified - emphasis added)*

We have all heard the greatest commandments:

> [37]*Jesus said to him, "'You shall love the LORD your God with all your heart, with all your soul, and with all your mind.'* [38]*This is the first and great commandment.* [39]*And the second is like it: 'You shall love your neighbor*

> *as yourself.' [40]On these two commandments*
> *hang all the Law and the Prophets."*
>   *Matthew 27:37-40 (NKJV)*

Later, when talking with his disciples, preparing them for the time that He would leave the earth, Jesus went on to say,

> *"[34]A new commandment I give to you,*
> *that you love one another; as I have loved*
> *you, that you also love one another. [35]By this*
> *all will know that you are My disciples, if you*
> *have love for one another."*
>   *John 13:34-35 (NKJV)*

The world is not supposed to know we are Christians by our stately churches, bumper stickers, protest rallies, or big leather Bibles. They are not impressed with that. What does impress the world is what they so lack: love for one another. John, who recorded the words of Jesus above, went on to write this well-known passage in his first letter,

> *[7]Beloved, let us love one another, for love*
> *is of God; and everyone who loves is born of*
> *God and knows God. [8]He who does not love*
> *does not know God, for God is love.*
>   *I John 4:7-8 (NKJV)*

So why are so many Christians today involved in disputes, lawsuits, and disagreements? They are not honoring God by obeying His commandment to walk in love.

I was privileged to participate in a marriage seminar given by Dr. Gary Chapman, best-selling author and host of the nationally-syndicated radio broadcast *A Growing Family.* The seminar was based on his best-selling book, *The Five Love Languages,* where he explained that different people give and receive love in different ways. Knowing your primary love language and the love language of your mate will help to better communicate the giving and receiving of love in your marriage. The idea that people are different is nothing new. Personality, preference, culture, and so much more make us diverse. Being able to express love in a way that is understood is a critical component to walking in love with one another and will cover a multitude of offenses. In his newest book, *Love as a Way of Life: 7 Traits That Will Transform Your Relationships,* Dr. Chapman explores ways to express love to others (not just our spouse), dealing with the qualities of Kindness, Patience, Forgiveness, Humility, Courtesy, Giving, and Honesty and how they can help us make love a way of life.

Until we make walking in love with one another a top priority, our organizations will continue to experience strife and enmity, losing cohesiveness and effectiveness. When we make love the "above all things" priority, we will be in position to be an effective organization and a testimony to the world.

God's Authority

Submission only begins at the point of disagreement. Yet so many Christians think they are submitting to God and Godly authority as long as they are in agreement with decisions made by those in leadership. We have all seen people who, when opposed to a decision made by the leadership of a church, suddenly were "called" to leave that church and go to another one, usually one more in keeping with their preference. I do not mean a disagreement over a moral issue, but a disagreement like the color of the carpet or hymnals or the like—not the decisions that decide eternity.

The Bible has much to say about Godly authority in the local church, in business, in the home, and in organizations. Unfortunately, too many Christians today are busy trying to have it their way, full of opinions and contention instead of service and love. God, speaking to Moses, called them stiff necked people (Exodus 32:9). In Psalm 81:12, God calls them stubbornhearted and walking in their own counsels. Jesus called these religious self-righteous people hypocrites, like white-washed tombs full of dead men's bones and all uncleanness (Matthew 23:27). Without going any further, I think it is easy to conclude that we do not want to be in that company! The end result is not very good either. Romans 2:5-8 in the Message Bible says,

The world is not supposed to know we are Christians by our stately churches, bumper stickers, protest rallies, or big leather Bibles. They are not impressed with that. What does impress the world is what they so lack: love for one another.

You're not getting by with anything. Every refusal and avoidance of God adds fuel to the fire. The day is coming when it's going to blaze hot and high, God's fiery and righteous judgment. Make no mistake: In the end you get what's coming to you—Real Life for those

who work on God's side, but to those who insist on getting their own way and take the path of least resistance, Fire!

Submission only begins at the point of disagreement.

I think that makes the point very well. God is not pleased with those who seek their own way and do not submit, either to His com-

mands or to the leadership that He establishes in the earth. In order for our organization to thrive, we must be submitted to God's plans carried out by those in leadership.

Additional study on this topic can be found in the following passages: Hebrews 13:7, Hebrews 13:17, Isaiah 1:19-20, Romans 13:1-2, I Samuel 15:23, and Galatians 5:19-21.

Handling Conflict

As long as Christians are breathing, there will be areas of conflict or disagreement. Disagreement is fine and we can agree to disagree; however, we must not be disagreeable to one another and unwilling to work together in unity. The Bible tells us to dwell in unity with all men as far as it concerns you.

[17]Repay no one evil for evil. Have regard for good things in the sight of all men. [18]If it is possible, as much as depends on you, live peaceably with all men. [19]Beloved, do not avenge yourselves, but rather give place to wrath; for it is written, "Vengeance is Mine, I will repay," says the Lord. [20]Therefore " If your enemy is hungry, feed him;

If he is thirsty, give him a drink;
For in so doing you will heap coals of fire
on his head."
    [21]Do not be overcome by evil, but over-
come evil with good.
                        Romans 12:17-21 (NKJV)

It amazes me to see what some would call mature Christians squabbling over the most trivial and eternally inconsequential things because of a personal, selfish agenda, refusing to prefer one another but demanding that others prefer them. The Bible sets a very clear standard in Romans 12:18: "If it is possible, as much as depends on you, live peaceably with all men." The requirement to live in peace is with us, not others. In Paul's second letter to Timothy, he deals with this issue in a very straightforward manner:

[22]Shun youthful lusts and flee from them,
and aim at and pursue righteousness (all that
is virtuous and good, right living, conformity
to the will of God in thought, word, and deed);
[and aim at and pursue] faith, love, [and]
peace (harmony and concord with others)
in fellowship with all [Christians], who call
upon the Lord out of a pure heart.
    [23]But refuse (shut your mind against, have
nothing to do with) trifling (ill-informed,
unedifying, stupid) controversies over igno-
rant questionings, for you know that they
foster strife and breed quarrels. [24]And the
servant of the Lord must not be quarrelsome
(fighting and contending). Instead, he must
be kindly to everyone and mild-tempered

[preserving the bond of peace]; he must be a skilled and suitable teacher, patient and forbearing and willing to suffer wrong. [25]He must correct his opponents with courtesy and gentleness, in the hope that God may grant that they will repent and come to know the Truth [that they will perceive and recognize and become accurately acquainted with and acknowledge it], [26]And that they may come to their senses [and] escape out of the snare of the devil, having been held captive by him, [henceforth] to do His [God's] will.

II Timothy 2:22-26 (Amplified)

Notice the emphasis at the end is on one thing: restoration. Whenever we face conflict with someone, our goal must always be restoration; restoration of the relationship with the overriding desire to be restoration of the other person's relationship with God.

When we are able to exhibit good leadership and maximize our intellectual, physical, spiritual, and organizational capacity, we can become that mature believer skilled in the word of righteousness described by Paul in Hebrews 5:14, and it can be said of us:

[9]But, beloved, we are confident of better things concerning you, yes, things that accompany salvation, though we speak in this manner. [10]For God is not unjust to forget your work and labor of love which you have shown toward His name, in that you have ministered to the saints, and do minister. [11]And we desire that each one of you show the same diligence

to the full assurance of hope until the end,
[12]that you do not become sluggish, but imitate
those who through faith and patience inherit
the promises.

Hebrews 6:9-12 (NKJV)

THE STORY (continued)
The Legacy Vision Retreat

Nathan and Eva got to the cabin early on Friday night to make sure everything was ready for the weekend. The cabin brought back so many wonderful memories with the family —summer vacations, ski trips, and even a few romantic weekend getaways for just the two of them. And painful memories, too. Like the time that Jennifer and Mariah came up for the weekend and Jennifer had to be rushed to the hospital after another "bad trip" from something she had used. Mariah was only three, but she still remembers it, too. Nathan and Eva certainly would like to have a vision for their future; they would be happy with just resolution.

When Luke arrived the next day, the three of them ate lunch together on the back porch. Eva's homemade chicken salad was still the best anywhere around, and the mountain air made everything taste more fresh. They talked casually over lunch about their upcoming weekend.

After lunch, Nathan and Eva got their questionnaire books that they had worked on at home. Luke began asking them to share their thoughts about the questions, one at a time. Initially the conversation was somewhat mechanical, but after a little while, the conversation seemed to come alive with memories, feelings, and some tears. They took a break for supper and went back into the conversation over dessert and coffee. Before they knew it, it was very late. Before they turned in for the night, Luke shared with them how well he thought they were doing and that he was looking forward to wrapping things up tomorrow.

The next morning was Sunday. Nathan, Eva and Luke enjoyed Nathan's famous blueberry pancakes for breakfast. After breakfast, Luke led them in a devotional time of Bible study and prayer. Afterwards, they rejoined their conversation from the night before. After a short break for lunch, they finished up a tiring but rewarding conversation of all of their questions, stories, dreams, goals, and visions. As Luke was preparing to leave, he told them that the next step was for Nathan and Eva to prepare their family legacy vision statement. Based on their conversations over the weekend, he would be able to help them draft it, but it would have to be their statement from their heart. They arranged a time to meet to go over this next step.

And with that, Nathan and Eva's weekend retreat was finished. Nathan and Eva were amazed to see how much they thought alike, even concerning things they had never discussed before. They were also amazed to see how the conversation grew with clarity and direction as they discovered what God had purposed for them. They were beginning to have hope that their lives would really matter, that the wealth they had acquired would not be squandered, but could be put to a valuable purpose to help their family and the kingdom of God. And that they could leave a legacy of values to their family as well. They could hardly wait to capture all of this in their family legacy vision statement to get closure on their past and provide direction for their future.

Financial Capital

Financial capital is that which God directs others to supply that we steward, use, and develop. It involves money, property, and other items that can be converted to currency to purchase goods and services. Financial capital includes all financial areas of a ministry, including the current operating budget as well as future funding. Most of the finance courses in Bible college or other ministry schools focus on Biblical principles, not specific practical steps and procedures to setting up and maintaining an operating budget or planning for future funding. These specific practical steps and procedures are critical to the success of every ministry and just as important as the underlying Biblical financial principles.

Current Funding

Current funding refers to the current operating budget, which includes projected revenues and expenses on a monthly, quarterly, annual and/or a multi-year basis and includes items such as staff salary and benefits, operating expenses, and overhead. God has much to say in His Word concerning business, which includes the business administration of ministry. Suffice it to say that waste is not a fruit of the Spirit. You should always know the condition of your "flock"—the resources entrusted to your administration.

Many gifted ministers in the five-fold ministry operate in functional gifts of leadership, teaching, and others, but do not have an aptitude for management or administration. That is where other peoples' gifts come into play, and it is especially critical in the areas of finance and administration. If you are not good at math and details, you do not need to be doing the bookkeeping and taxes for your ministry! If you do, it will not be long before you are facing a financial crisis—that is not prophesying doom; it is just understanding functional gifting. Two things: (1) make sure you manage well what you currently have in the bank and forecast in current income, and (2) make sure you make room in your budgeting for God to add provision for the mandates He has given you that are yet to be funded. If you do not make room for the provision, how can He bring it to you?

Future Funding

Future funding includes all areas commonly known as planned giving. This refers to money pledged, money given in trust, or some other arrangement for receiving known or unknown gifts of money or property in the future. This can be in the form of a ministry endowment or deferred gifts that will add to the future supply. The chapter on Tools and Techniques addresses many of these specific areas in greater detail.

Every ministry, no matter its current size or age, should be keeping an eye to the future financially. Jesus said,

> [28]*For which of you, intending to build a tower, does not sit down first and count the cost, whether he has enough to finish it—* [29]*lest, after he has laid the foundation, and is not able to finish, all who see it begin to mock him,* [30]*saying, "This man began to build and was not able to finish?"*
> Luke 14:28-30 (NKJV)

Without taking measures to plan for finances for the future, you are not "counting the cost" of the vision of your ministry or making room for those with the gift of giving who desire to leave their own legacy through your ministry. One with the gift of giving must function in their gift. Even if they are supposed to operate in their gift in partnership with your ministry, if your ministry is not able to facilitate that gift, they will have to seek out another ministry.

THE STORY (continued)
The Legacy Plan

Working with Luke, Nathan and Eva finished their family legacy vision statement and outlined their legacy planning goals. They met with their attorney and CPA to introduce Luke and to present their family legacy vision statement and their legacy planning goals. Their vision statement and goals would guide all of the planning that will develop their legacy. Their goals for their legacy plan are:

1. Provide a retirement income at their current standard of living plus inflation.
2. Transfer the family business to Chris with no taxation today or at Nathan and Eva's death.
3. Provide an equal inheritance for Jennifer in such a way that it will help her, not enable her.
4. Eliminate all estate taxes.
5. Provide a legacy fund for each of the grandchildren.
6. Leave a significant legacy gift for His Story Ministries.

After a few weeks, Luke finished designing Nathan and Eva's legacy plan. After reviewing the details with

---

them, Nathan and Eva were overwhelmed. Their goals were not just met but exceeded! Their income was more than they needed, they were able to pass control of the business to Chris now, they completely eliminated all estate taxes, and had plenty left over for a legacy fund for each of the grandchildren. But the most amazing part involved the planning for Jennifer. Luke showed them a way to set up a legacy trust for Jennifer that would allow her to have access to income from the trust as long as she met certain requirements such as being drug free and some other guidelines that Nathan and Eva agreed would help Jennifer. And if Jennifer needed food, clothing, shelter, medical help, rehab, or other physical assistance, the legacy trust would pay those expenses without giving Jennifer access to the money. No matter what choices Jennifer made, Nathan and Eva were helping their daughter, not enabling destructive behavior. Also, the legacy trust made sure that Mariah was cared for financially until she reached adulthood and was on her own. Nathan and Eva felt as if a heavy weight that they had carried for years was finally lifted.

Finally, Luke shared with Nathan and Eva the planning for His Story Ministries. Years earlier, Nathan had invested in several commercial buildings. His business outgrew each of them over time, but he kept them as rental property. They all had long-term leases that were generating substantial income that Nathan and Eva did not need in retirement. If they sold the properties, they would face substantial taxation on the sale. Luke showed them how they could donate the property to a deferred legacy trust. This trust would allow all of the income to to go to His Story Ministries over a period of twenty years and provide a sponsorship for students in the program. At the end of the twenty years, the property would pass to Nathan and Eva's children free of income, estate, or gift tax. To further personalize this trust, Luke recommended that they name the deferred legacy trust "Jenny's Fund" and dedicated the sponsorship on behalf of Jennifer.

Legacy Capital Summary

As mentioned above, the three types of capital in a legacy can be built and left to the next generation. It is the successful growth and development of this capital that leads to the accomplishment of the vision. Conversely, if a ministry fails to grow and develop any part of their legacy capital, either through ignorance, indifference, fear, or intentional neglect, the vision will not be accomplished in fullness by that ministry and may be passed to another.

If a ministry fails to grow and develop any part of their legacy capital, either through ignorance, indifference, fear, or intentional neglect, the vision will not be accomplished in fullness by that ministry and may be passed to another.

Jesus described the ways of the kingdom of God in how we handle capital entrusted to us in the parable of the servants found in Matthew 25. Although this may be a well-known parable, remember that we all have more to learn from God about His ways and His kingdom and still have room to develop our spiritual capacity. Read these words of Jesus with an open heart and open mind in light of the three forms of legacy capital.

> [14]*"For the kingdom of heaven is like a man traveling to a far country, who called his own servants and delivered his goods to them.* [15]*And to one he gave five talents, to another two, and to another one, to each according to his own ability; and immediately he went on a journey.* [16]*Then he who had received the five talents went and traded with them, and made another five talents.* [17]*And likewise he who had received two gained two more also.* [18]*But he who had received one went and dug in the ground, and hid his lord's money.* [19]*After a long time the lord of those servants came and settled accounts with them.*
>
> [20]*"So he who had received five talents came and brought five other talents, saying, 'Lord, you delivered to me five talents; look, I have gained five more talents besides them.'* [21]*His lord said to him, 'Well done, good and faithful servant; you were faithful over a few things, I will make you ruler over many things. Enter into the joy of your lord.'* [22]*He also who had received two talents came and said, 'Lord, you delivered to me two talents; look, I have gained two more talents besides them.'* [23]*His lord said to him, 'Well done, good and faithful servant; you have been faithful over a few things, I will make you ruler over many things. Enter into the joy of your lord.'* [24]*"Then he who had received the one talent*

came and said, 'Lord, I knew you to be a hard man, reaping where you have not sown, and gathering where you have not scattered seed. ²⁵And I was afraid, and went and hid your talent in the ground. Look, there you have what is yours.' ²⁶But his lord answered and said to him, 'You wicked and lazy servant, you knew that I reap where I have not sown, and gather where I have not scattered seed. ²⁷So you ought to have deposited my money with the bankers, and at my coming I would have received back my own with interest. ²⁸So take the talent from him, and give it to him who has ten talents.

²⁹'For to everyone who has, more will be given, and he will have abundance; but from him who does not have, even what he has will be taken away. ³⁰And cast the unprofitable servant into the outer darkness. There will be weeping and gnashing of teeth.'"

Matthew 25:14-30 (NKJV)

This is serious business! We are charged with growing and developing the capital of our legacy. Failure to do so has dire consequences. We all must pay great attention to how we handle our capital so that we can hear, "Well *done*, good and faithful servant; you were faithful over a few things, I will make you ruler over many things. Enter into the joy of your Lord."

> ## THE STORY (continued)
> ### *Wealthy for God*
>
> After some questions and quite a few tears, Nathan and Eva resolved to implement their legacy plan as soon as possible. Luke coordinated all of the steps with the other professionals needed and made sure none of the details were missed. Within a short time, they had all of the pieces of their legacy plan either in place or in the process. As they began working closely with His Story Ministries, Nathan and Eva found ways to help with the ministry. Eva taught some of the young women in a small group Bible study and even spent time showing some of them a few of her secret recipes, including her homemade chicken salad. Nathan helped with some of the work placement programs for the students, finding them jobs with local businesses.
>
> There were still many challenges ahead with transitioning the business to Chris and caring for Jennifer and Mariah, but now there was hope, a vision, and a plan. Nathan and Eva knew that this legacy plan did more than just accomplish their goals. It gave them a sense of purpose, a feeling that they had been missing for years, that what they did really made a difference. And it fulfilled their vision of leaving a meaningful legacy for generations to come. They finally knew what it meant to be *wealthy for God*.

Examples of Legacy

The Bible is full of examples of building and leaving a legacy—some Godly, some not. There are plenty of post-Biblical examples of Godly men and women who built and left a Godly legacy. Great writers have dealt with this topic; many of the stories have made it into plays and screenplays. The Christmas regular *It's A Wonderful Life* looks at the legacy built by George Bailey and the impact of one life on a whole community and even the world. Fiction, yes, but not so far from reality.

Jesus is, of course, the ultimate example of leaving a legacy. He mentored the twelve disciples for over three years and left them with instructions and a helper. That lasting legacy continues today and will throughout eternity. Below is a look into the lives and legacies of some fairly well-known figures in Biblical history. The purpose of the below illustrations is not to cover all of the aspects of their life, but to illustrate some key points concerning building and leaving a legacy.

Abraham and Isaac – The Covenant Legacy

In Genesis 12, God called Abraham out of his country to a land that God would show him. God promised to make him great, and He did! His holdings were so vast that he and Lot had to separate because the land could not support them both. After the birth of his long-awaited son, Isaac, Abraham faced the greatest test of his life: giving up his long-awaited son. All he had was God's promise that his son would produce a family greater than the stars in the sky. Instead of teaching Isaac fear and disobedience, Abraham took Isaac to sacrifice on an altar. At the moment that Abraham was drawing the knife to slay his son, the Angel of the LORD stopped him. Abraham found a ram in the bushes and declared the name of the place to be Jehovah Jireh: The LORD Will See and Provide.

Abraham's legacy was passed to Isaac and later to all who would enter into his covenant through Jesus:

> *And if you are Christ's, then you are Abraham's seed, and heirs according to the promise.*
>
> *Galatians 3:29 (NKJV)*

Abraham's legacy continues today—a legacy rich in spiritual, human, and financial capital.

Lessons Learned From Abraham and Isaac

Faithfulness to the vision is critical in the face of delays and seemingly insurmountable obstacles. Faithfulness above all else leads to the successful passing of your ministry's leagacy to your successor.

Moses and Joshua – The Leadership Legacy

Moses, the adopted kid who made it big, went through his desert experience to become the humble servant of the great I Am. Successfully leading the exodus from slavery, he brought hope and a new future to former slaves. Moses became one of the greatest leaders in Israel's history, leading them from harsh slavery to the Promised Land flowing with milk and honey. Throughout the exodus, he groomed his protégé, Joshua. When Joshua was sent to spy out the land, he was one of the two who said, "we are well able," capturing the vision of Moses. From that point, he went on to shadow Moses throughout the forty years in the wilderness. As his minister/assistant, Moses chose Joshua to lead the famous battle against Amalek, where Aaron and Hur held up Moses' hands. As a capable worshipper in the temple and a commander in battle, Joshua was developing in the skills necessary to continue Moses' legacy.

Incidentally, the legacy of generations of slavery was so powerful that none of the slave generation was able to break free from it and enter into the Promised Land other than Joshua and Caleb. Caleb and Joshua had one advantage over the others—they had seen the future and embraced it. They were determined to build a new legacy.

As Moses reached the end of his days, the LORD took Moses up to Mount Abarim to see the land that he would not be allowed to enter. Moses asked the LORD to set a man over the congregation. The LORD told Moses that He has chosen Joshua, "a man in whom is the Spirit" (Numbers 27:18), and that Moses was to inaugurate Joshua before the people. At Moses' death, the LORD instructs Joshua to lead the people into the Promised Land. Of course, the rest is history. Moses spent over forty years grooming Joshua for this task. The end result: a Spirit-led warrior leader who laid hold of the inheritance of the children of Israel. Moses built and successfully transferred the legacy of leadership to Joshua, the able new leader of a nation descended from slaves.

Lessons Learned From Moses and Joshua
Never faint in your pursuit of your God-given vision. Instead, trust that God is continually developing you to fulfill the vision.

Rahab – The Redeemed Legacy

Rahab the harlot lived in Jericho. One day, Joshua, the new leader of the Israelites, sent out two spies to view the land, especially Jericho (Joshua 2). The king of Jericho heard that the spies were in town staying at Rahab's house. When the king asked Rahab to bring the spies, she said that they had escaped in the night and that the king should send out men to catch them. Actually, Rahab hid the men on her roof under stalks of flax. When she returned, she told the spies that she knew that the LORD had given them the land, and after all the stories of the LORD drowning the Egyptians in the Red Sea and the Israelite's military victories, all the people of Jericho had been fearfully waiting to be next. She made a deal with the spies to save her family since she had helped them.

When the spies returned to Joshua, they reported that all of Jericho was in a panic over their impending doom. Later, when the Israelites crossed over the Jordan, they planned their attack on Jericho. Joshua gave them instructions for the famous silent march around Jericho. I can only imagine the fear that built in the minds of the people of Jericho. On the seventh day when the wall fell, Joshua sent the same two spies to rescue Rahab and her family. Everyone else in Jericho was killed and the city burned. Because Rahab helped the two spies, she and her family escaped the devastation and lived in peace in the land of Israel.

Later on, Rahab married an Israelite named Salmon. They had a son named Boaz. You may recall that he married a foreigner named Ruth. They had a son named Jesse who had a son named David. He became the great warrior king of Israel. After quite a few more "begots," David's lineage led to Joseph who married Mary and raised Jesus. Rahab is mentioned in Hebrews 11:31 in the Hall of Fame of Faith because she, by faith, received the spies with peace. Her act of faith took her from being a harlot of Jericho to the great-grandmother of King David and in the lineage of Jesus the Messiah. That is a legacy redeemed!

Lessons Learned From Rahab
Your legacy depends more on the choices you make today and in the future than the choices you have made in the past. If you want a different legacy than the one you are currently developing, make a change today. God is in the redeeming business and is well able to redeem your leagcy.

Elijah and Elisha – The Prophetic Legacy

Elijah was a hard-nosed prophet of God. His no-nonsense approach is best exemplified when he challenged the prophets of Baal that had taken over the spiritual rule of God's people. His one-liner asking the Baalan prophets why their god would not answer is a classic:

> *About noontime Elijah began mocking them. "You'll have to shout louder," he scoffed, "for surely he is a god! Perhaps he is daydreaming, or is relieving himself. Or maybe he is away on a trip, or is asleep and needs to be wakened!"*
> *I Kings 18:27 (New Living Translation)*

When the contest ended and God had consumed Elijah's offering, Elijah had the people round up the 450 prophets of Baal and he killed them all! And if that was not enough, he then prayed to God until the rain came and ended the drought that Elijah has previously prophesied. That is a no-nonsense prophet!

After a time of seeking the LORD in the wilderness, the LORD told him to anoint Elisha as the next prophet to replace Elijah. When Elijah found Elisha, Elisha was farming.

> *[19]So he departed from there, and found Elisha the son of Shaphat, who was plowing with twelve yoke of oxen before him, and he was with the twelfth. Then Elijah passed by him and threw his mantle on him. [20]And he left the oxen and ran after Elijah, and said, "Please let me kiss my father and my mother, and then I will follow you." And he said to him, "Go back again, for what have I done to you?" [21]So Elisha turned back from him, and took a yoke of oxen and slaughtered them and boiled their flesh, using the oxen's equipment, and gave it to the people, and they ate. Then he arose and followed Elijah, and became his servant.*
>
> *1 Kings 19:19-21 (NKJV)*

Elisha did not make any provision for reversing his commitment to Elijah; instead he killed the oxen and burned the plow. That is commitment!

Elisha apparently lived a very humble life of service with Elijah. When Jehosophat, king of Judah, was asking for a prophet of the LORD, one of the servants of the king of

Israel tells King Jehosophat about Elisha, describing him as *"Elisha the son of Shaphat is here, who poured water on the hands of Elijah" (II Kings 3:11 NKJV)*—a rather unspectacular reputation.

At the end of his service to Elijah, Elisha had witnessed Elijah operating in his office of prophet from challenging sin in the lives of the kings of Israel and prophesying their death to literally calling down fire from heaven to consume over 100 soldiers. When Elijah was traveling to the place where he would be taken into heaven, Elisha stayed by his side until the end. When Elijah asked Elisha what he wanted from Elijah before he was taken to heaven, Elisha asked for a double portion of Elijah's spirit.

> *[11]Then it happened, as they continued on and talked, that suddenly a chariot of fire appeared with horses of fire, and separated the two of them; and Elijah went up by a whirlwind into heaven. [12]And Elisha saw it, and he cried out, "My father, my father, the chariot of Israel and its horsemen!" So he saw him no more. And he took hold of his own clothes and tore them into two pieces.*
> *II Kings 2:11-12 (NKJV)*

After Elijah departed in the whirlwind, Elisha picked up Elijah's mantle and stepped into his office.

Throughout his time as prophet, Elisha prophesied droughts and famines, deliverance during a siege, and performed many miracles of provision and healing, carrying on the legacy of Elijah. One interesting commonality occurs at the end of Elisha's life. *"Elisha had become sick with the illness of which he would die. Then Joash the king of Israel came down to him, and wept over his face, and said, 'O my father, my father, the chariots of Israel and their horsemen!'"* (II Kings 13:14) These are the same words Elisha cried out at Elijah's departure.

In the spring after Elisha was buried, a group was burying another man when a group of Moabite raiders approached. In their haste, they placed the dead man in Elisha's tomb. When the dead man touched Elisha's bones, the dead man revived and stood up. Even after his death, the double portion lived on!

Lessons Learned From Elijah and Elisha
One of the best roads to achieve greatness is the road of dedicated service. Elisha's faithful service qualified him to carry on the legacy and increase in it. Self promotion will never lead to true success. Psalm 75 shares that promotion comes from the Lord. Trust in Him and apply yourself to dedicated service to the ministry He has placed before you and let Him exalt you.

Elisha and Gehazi – The Lost Legacy

Like Elisha was to Elijah, Gehazi was the servant to Elisha. The only mention of Gehazi's origin is found in II Kings 4 in the story of the Shunammite woman and her son, and he is merely referred to as Gehazi, [Elisha's] servant. No dramatic killing of oxen. No impactful scene of dedication to Elisha. Just Gehazi the servant. Unlike Elisha's humble service and little known history leading to his ordination as a prophet, the Bible tells us much about Gehazi's service to Elisha.

Gehazi was the liaison for Elisha. He was sent to talk to the Shunammite woman in II Kings 4 and he later was sent with Elisha's staff to lay it on her dead son. Gehazi was sent to talk to the Syrian army commander, Naaman, who came to Elisha seeking healing of leprosy and was trusted to carry the message of the terms of the healing.

Even after seeing all of the powerful miracles performed through Elisha, Gehazi did not have a reverence for God or for the prophet of God. This is most telling in the story of Naaman in II Kings 5. Naaman had heard of Elisha through a servant girl from Israel. Naaman was sent to Elisha by the king of Syria along with lots of gold, silver, and clothing. After following Elisha's instructions through Gehazi, Naaman was healed of leprosy. Naaman offered all of these valuables to Elisha in gratitude for his healing. Elisha refused to take any of the valuables. After he left, Gehazi, the one who Naaman recognized as the official liaison, pursued Naaman, made up a lie about Elisha needing some of the goods after all, and made off with a load of silver and clothing that he took back home and hid. That was, of course, a very dumb move for Gehazi, trying to sneak around his master, who happens to be a bona fide prophet of God. When Elisha asked Gehazi where he had been, of course Gehazi lies that he has been nowhere. Here is Elisha's reply:

> *[26]But Elisha asked him, "Don't you realize that I was there in spirit when Naaman stepped down from his chariot to meet you? Is this the time to receive money and clothing, olive groves and vineyards, sheep and cattle, and male and female servants? [27]Because you have done this, you and your descendants will suffer from Naaman's leprosy forever."*

> *When Gehazi left the room, he was covered*
> *with leprosy; his skin was white as snow.*
> *II Kings 5:26-27 (NKJV)*

Little more is said about Gehazi. No transfer of the mantle. No double portion. No bones that raise a corpse back to life. Not even a good prophetic warning. Nothing. Gehazi failed to take ownership of the legacy that was available to him. This is, unfortunately, still a problem with too many ministries today. Leaving a legacy is not just about providing a vision for someone to admire. It is bringing the successor into the vision before departure. Elisha took hold of the vision, placing a demand on Elijah to pass the legacy to him. Gehazi disqualified himself by trying to deceptively obtain a small portion of a legacy that was not his to take. I wonder what great things would have happened in Elisha's legacy if Gehazi would have met the requirements to receive the legacy.

Lessons Learned From Elisha and Gehazi
Gehazi lost his opportunity to continue Elisha's legacy as a result of his focus on greedy personal gain instead of submission to his spiritual leader. Never let your focus shift to greed and personal gain at the expense of the ministry. Do not become so familiar with the operation of the ministry that you lose your reverence for the ministry, the ones you serve, and the One who called you.

Paul and Timothy – The Ministerial Legacy

Paul was not always the great apostle and leader of the church. He was at one time its arch enemy. Paul, who was born Saul of Tarsus, was a student of Gamaliel, one of the leading Hebrew teachers of the time. He knew the scriptures and was zealous to enforce them, even to the point of searching out and imprisoning those of the Way, the followers of Jesus Christ, regarding them as heretics of the faith. Then, when on the road to Damascus to seek out more Christians to persecute, he had an encounter with the Way: Jesus Himself.

After the Damascus road conversion, Paul spent about three years developing his new legacy before he even approached the Christians in Jerusalem. When he attempted to join up with church leaders in Jerusalem, they would not receive him for fear of his reputation in persecuting Christians. After Paul proved himself, he joined the missionary outreach of the early church.

On one of his trips to Lystra, he met Timothy. Timothy was well thought of by the believers in Lystra, and Paul took Timothy with him and Silas on their missionary trip. From that rather uneventful meeting grew a friendship and father-son relationship that is unparalleled in the New Testament. Paul was so taken with Timothy's ability and desire to capture Paul's heart that he sent Timothy to Philippi:

> *[20]I have no one else like Timothy, who genuinely cares about your welfare. [21]All the others care only for themselves and not for what matters to Jesus Christ. [22]But you know how Timothy has proved himself. Like a son with his father, he has served with me in preaching the Good News.*
>
> *Philippians 2:20-22 (NKJV)*

While Paul is in prison, Timothy becomes Paul's eyes, ears, hands, and heart to the churches. Being sent from church to church on Paul's behalf, Timothy had become an extension of Paul, not just an associate.

Paul places Timothy as pastor/bishop of Ephesus to make sure that the purity of the Gospel is maintained. In his letters to Timothy, he gives advice, exhortation, instruction, and admonition to Timothy, continuing the mentoring process until the end. Timothy has been chosen, instructed, tested, and proven worthy of the legacy that began on the road to Damascus so many years prior. Paul summarizes his work with Timothy in his charge to Timothy just before his own death:

> *²Preach the word! Be ready in season and out of season. Convince, rebuke, exhort, with all longsuffering and teaching. ³For the time will come when they will not endure sound doctrine, but according to their own desires, because they have itching ears, they will heap up for themselves teachers; ⁴and they will turn their ears away from the truth, and be turned aside to fables. ⁵But you be watchful in all things, endure afflictions, do the work of an evangelist, fulfill your ministry.*
> *II Timothy 4:2-5 (NKJV)*

Like never before, we seem to be in that time mentioned in verse three, yet the impact of Paul's legacy through Timothy has kept the church on course for nearly two thousand years.

Lessons Learned From Paul and Timothy
Always seek to groom successors, the ones who will carry on your legacy. Someone once said that success without a successor is a failure. Pouring your time and energy into those who share your heart and vision is critical to the successful continuation of your legacy.

Final Thoughts on Legacy

What will your ministry's legacy be? Do you have a vision for it? Is it God's vision for you? Too many people are creating plans and asking God to bless them. That is not how He operates. Instead, ask Him what His plan is for you and get about doing it. Stop and take the time to get alone with God and ask him to show you the vision of His desired legacy for you and your ministry.

Once you have His vision, do a thorough capital assessment. Be sure you know what you have and what you still need in order to bring the vision to pass. You can use the Capital Assessment in the Appendix to make sure you do not miss any critical areas.

Sharing the Vision

Now for the best part: sharing your vision. The optimal legacy is best achieved by the successful blending of the resources of the ministry (the working) with the resources of the giver (the sending) around a common vision. There are people who God has called to work with you, each according to their functional gifting, helping you bring the vision to pass. God has already placed inside of them a desire that matches the vision He placed in you.

The optimal legacy is best achieved by the successful blending of the resources of the ministry (the working) with the resources of the giver (the sending) around a common vision.

Many of these have achieved success in their lives and are seeking significance: significance of work, significance of giving, and significance of purpose. These people, seeking to move from making a living to having an abundant life are often the ones most interested in their legacy and most ready to help you achieve your vision. In order to complete your mandates, build and leave a legacy, you must connect with these people. Share your vision with the ones that God brings across your path and allow God to draw them to the vision.

A Clear Vision Statement Is Essential

Martin Luther King's most memorable speech included the words, "I have a dream...." where he cast his vision for a day when his children would live in a nation where they would not be judged by the color of their skin but by the content of their character. That stirring speech was given at the Lincoln memorial, a memorial to the president who began the end of slavery, adding further context to the vision. He painted a vision, a clear vision. It was more than a statement of his personal wishes; it was a call to action. Those who shared that vision rallied behind him; those who disagreed with that vision moved away from him.

Vision should never be mediocre or commonplace; the sharing of the vision should never be tenative or vague. A well-stated vision should always provoke. Those who share the vision should be provoked to join in; those who have a different vision should be able to easily recognize that there is not a match. For example, "Do good for humanity" is not clear. It neither attracts nor repels. "Remove hunger from the daily experience of the displaced peoples of Darfur" is, on the other hand, a clear statement of deliberate action, a large undertaking, that will specifically affect a clearly-identifiable segment of humanity by meeting a tangible life need. That is a vision statement that could act as a rallying cry to those who want to see its fulfillment.

Finance Your Vision While Meeting a Need

In order for your ministry to build and leave a legacy, it needs money. This is the tangible and interdependent need for the ministry and the gift of giving. As mentioned earlier, it is God's design to have the two work together, each helping meet the need of the other. Up to now, we have explored the spiritual needs and the vision needs for the giver. Just like the ministry, the giver also has legacy needs.

The giver's legacy needs include leaving an inheritance for his or her children's children, giving efficiently and effectively, tax reduction, business continuation, and passing virtues and values to the next generation along with the financial value of their estate.

When designed and implemented properly, solutions that help the giver to build and leave a legacy can also help meet the financial needs of a ministry to build and leave its legacy. In other words, this whole concept of interdependence extends beyond the spiritual needs of the giver and financial needs of the ministry; it extends into the legacy needs of the giver and the ministry. The ministry and the giver have the need to leave their vision (spiritual capital) to their successor (human capital) with sufficient finances 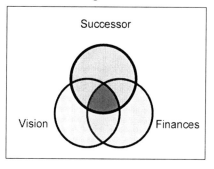 (financial capital) to grow the vision. Successfully merging these distinct yet interdependent parts of the legacy leads to the optimal legacy plan, both for the giver and the ministry.

The next section will help you, the ministry, become familiar with many of the basic tools and designs used in legacy planning. Knowing the need for this interdependency and being familiar with some of the tools and designs used in legacy planning can enable the ministry to better assist the giver with his legacy needs.

Chapter 4

Building and Leaving a Legacy: The Construction Guide

He is like a man building a house, who dug down deep and laid the foundation on rock. When a flood came, the torrent struck that house but could not shake it, because it was well built.

Luke 6:48 (NIV)

Before you delve into this section, it is important to understand why this information is essential for you to know in your role as a ministry. This section is not intended to make you an expert in legacy planning, but to familiarize you with some of the strategies used to effectively build and leave a legacy. Awareness leads to identification which leads to implementation. Being aware of these strategies will help you better identify people with the gift of giving and identify opportunities to help them unleash their gift. In other words, once you identify an opportunity, you can work with the giver and the legacy advisor to optimize the planning for the ministry and the giver.

The Building Supplies: The Major Forms of Giving

Most people are familiar with the most common method of giving giving: outright gifts of cash. There are many forms of giving, both current and deferred. Having a firm understanding of the different types of giving allows the ministry and the giver to work together to increase efficiency and effectiveness of the gift.

Current Giving

Outright Gifts of Cash

If you understand what you are looking for, you will have a much greater probability of finding it.

Outright gifts of cash to a ministry enables the giver to support the current mission and service of a ministry and may qualify for a charitable income tax deduction for givers who itemize their deductions. A giver will receive a charitable tax deduction for the full amount of their contribution. Outright gifts can be used to provide current support, establish an endowment, or underwrite a special project for a ministry. The charitable deduction can be taken in the year of the gift. If the value of the gift exceeds the annual limit for deductibility, the remaining amount can be carried forward for five more years.

> **Example: An Outright Gift.** Sam and Margie Smith are members of First Church in their town. The church is in the middle of a building project. The Smiths have been contributing to the project for several years and have always wanted to give more. The Smiths contributed $250,000 to their church, completing the building project. They were able to take the full $250,000 as a tax deduction, but because of their adjusted gross income, they could only use $150,000 in the year of the gift. They carried the remaining $100,000 forward and were able to use the remaining amount of charitable deduction in future years.

Appreciated Property

Appreciated property is property that has grown in value above its original purchase price (the basis) and can include securities, real estate, etc. The giver gifts the asset to the ministry. The full value of the gift is fully deductible. The giver can take the tax deduction in the year of the gift up to 30% of adjusted gross income and any remaining amount of the deduction can be carried over for an additional five years. In addition to the tax deduction, the giver avoids capital gains tax on the appreciation.

> **Example: A Gift of Appreciated Property.** Donald and Helen Turner have shares of stock that have grown in value from their original $50,000 investment to $150,000, a $100,000 capital gain. They would like to donate $150,000 to a local school for at-risk children. If they sell the stock, they will owe federal capital gain tax and state income tax of $22,750. If they donate the remaining value of

the stock, their total donation would be $127,250 with a resulting charitable deduction for the gift.

Given that the Turners are in the 40% combined federal and state tax bracket, their deduction would save them $50,900. The total value of the gift and the deduction is $127,250 + $50,900 = $178,150. If instead the Turners gave the stock directly to the school, the school could sell the stock with no taxable gain, thereby keeping the full $150,000. Also, the Turners will receive a corresponding deduction for the full $150,000, resulting in a tax savings of $60,000. Total value of the gift of the stock: $150,000 + $60,000 = $210,000, an increase of $31,850, an 18% increase in value.

Charitable Bargain Sale

If a giver has an asset that they sell below market value to a ministry, in essence creating a bargain for the ministry, the difference between the fair market value and the sale price is tax deductible to the giver. For example, if the property is appreciated real estate, the tax deduction could be used to lessen or neutralize the tax impact on the gain from the sale.

Example: A Charitable Bargain Sale. Betty Jones has a piece of investment property that she was given by her father. At the time he bought it, the property was valued at $5,000. Now nearly 40 years later, the property is valued at approximately $500,000. If she could sell the property for $500,000, she will realize a capital gain of $495,000, resulting in a combined federal and state tax of over $112,500, leaving Betty with $340,000 after the taxes and realtor have been paid. The land is next to her church, and she would like to give it to them, but she needs the money from the sale. If instead she sells the land directly to the church for $400,000, she will reduce the capital gain to $395,000 and she will generate a charitable tax deduction of $100,000 for the difference between the $500,000 value of the land and the $400,000 sale price. Considering that the tax deduction is against all income, not just capital gains, her total tax savings from the deduction will be $35,750 given her other income and tax situation, and the tax on the gain will be $89,800. After the sale is completed, Betty will have $345,900 on the sale, $5,900 more than selling it outright, and she will have given her church a $100,000 savings on the land.

Deferred Giving

Bequest

This is the simplest form and the most well-known method of deferred giving. A giver wants to do something meaningful for a ministry at his or her death and names the ministry as a beneficiary. At the death of the giver, the ministry receives the gift. The value of the bequest is deductible by the estate for federal estate and income tax purposes.

Charitable Gift of Life Insurance

Similar to the bequest above, a giver names a ministry as a beneficiary of a life insurance death benefit. If the giver transfers the ownership of the policy to the ministry, the giver will receive a current charitable tax deduction for the value of the policy and future premium payments made. At the giver's death, the ministry receives the death benefit from the policy. Depending on the giver's health and age at the time the policy is issued, the death benefit could be considerably more than the premium paid, multiplying the value of the gift.

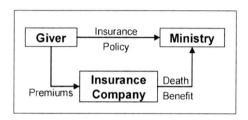

Example: A Charitable Gift of Life Insurance. Neil Owens wants to leave a large gift to his home church. Neil is retired and in great health, but he does not have a large sum of extra money that he can leave to his church. At 62 years old, Neil is receiving an extra $35,000 per year for the next 10 years due to a deferred compensation arrangement from his former employer. Neil contacts the church and sets up a Charitable Gift of Life Insurance. He agrees to donate $31,000 to the church annually for ten years and the church will, in turn, purchase a life insurance policy on his life. Because of his age and health, the church is able to purchase a $1,000,000 guaranteed life insurance policy on Neil's life and it will be paid up in 10 years when Neil's extra retirement income ends. Neil receives a $31,000 income tax deduction annually for his gift to the church and the church receives $1,000,000 at Neil's death, more than three times Neil's total annual gifts of $310,000.

Remainder Interest in Home or Farm

If a giver owns a home or farm, he or she can give that home or farm to a ministry while retaining the right to continue living there (life estate) for his or her life. The home can include a second home. The giver gets a charitable tax deduction for the ministry's remainder interest, the future value of the gift based on life expectancy of the giver. At the death of the giver, the ministry receives the full ownership of the home or farm.

Example: Remainder Interest in Home. Joanne Preston lives next door to her church. She and her late husband, Dwight, built the house just after they were married and raised their family in the house. Now at 75 years old, her two sons and her daughter have families of their own and live out of town. Dwight started a Boy Scout troop at the church over forty years ago and that troop is still going strong. Both of her sons became Eagle Scouts in that troop and she has always maintained a close relationship with all of the Scoutmasters since Dwight "retired" from Scouting over twenty years ago. When Dwight passed away, Joanne wanted to do something special for the troop. After meeting with the Scoutmaster, Troop Committee, and representatives from the church, Joanne decided to donate her house at her death for the troop to use for its Scouting program. Instead of leaving the house in her will, she decides to give the remainder interest to the troop now and maintain the right to live in the house for her lifetime. At her death, the troop would get the Dwight Preston Memorial Scout Hut. Joanne's house appraises for $300,000 and the current value of the remainder interest is $191,000, which Joanne receives as a tax deduction now.

Pooled Income Fund

A pooled income fund is a ministry-sponsored fund that allows givers to donate into the fund and receive a proportionate share of the income of the fund annually. The giver receives a charitable tax deduction equal to the remainder interest of the gift, and receives an income for life. The givers can make subsequent contributions to the fund. After the death of the giver, the funds given are released to the ministry. The benefits of the pooled income fund include:

1. The giver receives an income for life.
2. The giver receives a charitable tax deduction.
3. Appreciated property avoids tax on the capital gain.
4. The income to the giver may be more than the asset is providing them before the gift.

Example: A Pooled Income Fund. Anthony and Maria Russo are about to retire. Anthony, 67, and Maria, 65 need extra income for retirement. Maria has a stock portfolio that was given to her by her late father. The portfolio is currently valued at $100,000, and Maria's father started the portfolio many years ago with just $5,000. If the Russos sell the stock, they will face capital gains tax on the $95,000 gain, resulting in less money to use for income. The Russos heard that one of the ministries they support has a pooled income fund. After exploring the option with the ministry, they decide to donate the stock portfolio to the fund. As a result, the stock is sold with no capital gains tax for the Russos and they will receive a lifetime income from the fund based on the fund's performance and a current tax deduction of over $30,000.

Charitable Gift Annuity

A charitable gift annuity (CGA) is a contractual agreement between a giver and a ministry. The giver makes an irrevocable gift to the ministry, often an appreciated asset. In exchange for the gift, the ministry agrees to pay a fixed amount of income periodically for life to the giver. The income can be paid to an individual or to two recipients (annuitants) and can begin immediately or be deferred for a set amount of time. For tax purposes, the gift is treated as part gift and part annuity purchase. Therefore, the charitable deduction for the gift is reduced by the value of the annuity. Also, the income received is treated as part taxable income and part tax-free return of original principal.

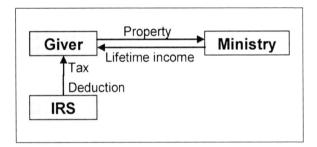

The benefits of a charitable gift annuity include:

1. The giver receives an income for life.
2. The income can be immediate or deferred.
3. The giver receives a charitable tax deduction.
4. Any capital gain tax liability on appreciated property is spread out over the life expectancy of the annuitant.
5. The income to the giver may be more than the asset is providing them before the gift.
6. It is easy to understand and implement.

Example: A Charitable Gift Annuity. Luis and Juanita Martinez are retiring in two years. Over the past several years, they have acquired and managed several rental properties. They have considered selling the properties and giving up the responsibility of property management, but they purchased most of the properties many years ago and between increasing values and depreciation taken on their taxes, there would be considerable taxes due on the sale of the properties. While volunteering at a local rescue mission, Juanita mentions their dilemma to the director who tells her about their gift annuity program. Luis and Juanita meet with the director a week later and discover that they can donate their $5,000,000 worth of rental property to the rescue mission, avoid all capital gains and depreciation recovery tax, and receive a lifetime income of 5.3% of the $5,000,000, $265,000 per year, beginning in two years when they retire. And, over half of their annual income will be tax-free for the first 25 years. And Luis and Juanita will receive a tax deduction of over $1,200,000 for the gift.

Charitable Remainder Trust – The Full Income Trust

One of the most popular advanced forms of deferred giving, a Charitable Remainder Trust (CRT), is similar to the CGA above. The CRT is an irrevocable trust that allows a giver to donate property to a trust, receive an income for life, receive an income tax deduction for the value of the remainder that will go to a ministry, and avoid capital gains tax on the sale of the property inside the tax-free trust. At the death of the giver, the remainder property will go to the named ministry or ministries. This is an ideal method to consider for the giver who has a highly-appreciated low-income property, such as real estate, who wants more income without selling the property and thereby realizing a taxable gain on the sale. If the asset were sold outside the trust, the value of the asset would be reduced by taxation, thereby reducing the amount available to generate income. Because the asset is sold tax-free inside the trust, the full value of the asset can be used to generate income.

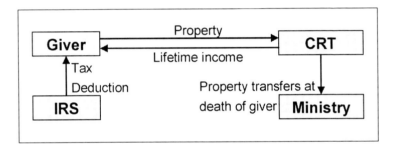

Benefits of a Charitable Remainder Trust are similar to the CGA, but the CRT has much greater flexibility:

1. The CRT can be established during the life of the giver or can be set up at death (testamentary).
2. The giver can choose a fixed income payout (charitable remainder annuity trust or CRAT) or can choose a variable payout as a percent of the value of the trust (charitable remainder unitrust or CRUT).
3. Within certain limits, the giver can select the payout rate of the trust.
4. Income can be paid to multiple beneficiaries for life, in succession.
5. The giver can be the trustee or can hire a trustee and change that trustee if they so choose.

6. The trustee decides how the investments are handled, not the ministry.
7. The income paid to the giver is taxable based on the four-tier system of taxation.
8. The ministry remainder beneficiary can be changed during the giver's life.
9. The remainder beneficiary can be a foundation controlled by the giver's family.

Example: A Charitable Remainder Trust. Paul and Linda Miller are 60 years old and own Better Breads, a regional natural grains bread company. Paul's father gave him the business over thirty years ago. They never had children and do not have any family interested in taking over the business. They have been approached for years by a competitor who would like to purchase their company, but Paul and Linda were not ready to give up the company. Now as they approach retirement, they are considering selling the company. Better Breads is valued at over $4,000,000, but with the low basis of the company stock, Paul and Linda would have to give up over $1,000,000 to taxes upon the sale. Paul and Linda consult with their accountant who refers them to a legacy advisor. She shows them how they can donate the company stock to a Charitable Remainder Trust, avoid all of the capital gains on the sale of the business, and generate a lifetime income for retirement. And when Paul and Linda pass away, the funds left in the trust can go to their favorite ministries. When the company sells, they can receive a lifetime income of 7% of the value of the assets in the trust. In addition to avoiding all of the capital gains taxes and receiving a lifetime income, they also will receive a tax deduction of over $680,000.

Charitable Lead Trust – The Timed Inheritance Trust

The Charitable Lead Trust (CLT) is the opposite of the CRT. In this case, the giver gives away the income to the ministry and keeps the asset in the family. This is like making a temporary gift, loaning the asset to the ministry to use for a set period of time.

For givers who want to keep property in the family but do not need the income, this is an ideal form of giving to a ministry. The value of the income paid to the ministry is tax deductible for federal gift and estate tax purposes, thereby

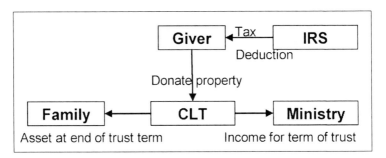

reducing the value of the remainder interest of the CLT. Because of this, the CLT is often used to reduce the potential gift or estate tax on transferring an asset to the next generation. When properly designed, the giver can give the asset to the next generation by giving it through a ministry and avoid all gift and estate taxes on the value of the asset. Not only can the transfer avoid gift and estate taxes, the giver also avoids any tax on the appreciation of the property while it is "on loan" to the ministry.

> **Example: A Charitable Lead Trust.** Charles and Susan Jackson are retired. They have a large estate that is subject to estate taxes and they are currently receiving more taxable income than they need for their lifestyle. They own a commercial building worth $1,400,000 that is generating nearly $100,000 per year in excess income. They decide to donate the building to a Charitable Lead Annuity Trust (CLAT) to reduce their taxable income and estate. They set up the trust for a term of 25 years. Over the next 25 years, their favorite ministries will receive the nearly $100,000 of annual income to fund their ongoing needs. At the end of that time, the building will pass to their heirs free from estate and income tax.

Alternative Vehicles for Giving: Foundations

Foundations can be described as an entity acting on behalf of a giver—a giving institution. There are many types of foundations and as many reasons for setting them up. Some foundations are used to consolidate giving, some are used to simplify giving, and some are used to share the joys and responsibilities of giving. Whatever the reason, foundations can be used as an extension of giving for individuals, families, and communities, including communities based on geographic location and communities based on ideas and beliefs.

Private Foundation – Hands-On Control

A private foundation is a charitable organization largely controlled by the giver, subject to legal limitations. These private foundations allow the giver to have great control over their gifts. The foundation can do or fund charitable work directly, meeting the needs of individuals and groups. The increased flexibility and control is offset by lower deductibility limits – 30% of adjusted growth income (AGI) per year for regular contributions and 20% for appreciated property, unless the foundation meets more restrictive criteria for its operation. There are additional restrictions imposed on private foundations, including prohibited transactions between the foundation and giver, certain investments, distribution minimum requirements, and more. If the giver really desires great control and flexibility, it may outweigh the limitations.

Supporting Organization – The Distribution Center

A supporting organization is a foundation that is treated as a public charity. A supporting organization can be established and controlled by the giver and his or her family. As the name implies, the supporting organization's structure allows only for support of other public ministries. The supporting organization does not afford the ability to do charitable works of service such as direct help to individuals in need, but does allow contributions to established nonprofit ministries that directly help individuals. Similar to a commercial distribution center, the supporting organization receives contributions and distributes them to ministries much like a wholesale distributor would distribute their products to a store where they can be purchased by the consumer.

Donor-Advised Funds – The Charitable Bank Account

A donor-advised fund (DAF) is maintained at a charitable organization. The giver does not have the ability to control or restrict the use of the funds, but has the ability to recommend, or advise on, distributions from the fund for charitable purposes, hence the name donor-*advised* funds. The giver's contributions are treated as a donation to a public charity for tax purposes.

Some financial services companies have begun to offer charitable funds that are similar to donor-advised funds. These "gift funds" operate similarly to the DAF, but allow the giver more control over their investment of funds by choosing which company's gift fund they want to use.

Donor-advised funds offer the giver benefits including:

1. An immediate tax deduction that can help manage taxes from year to year.
2. Flexibility in choosing ministries after making the gift.
3. Potentially lower administrative burden and cost of management than a supporting organization.
4. Better tax deductibility limitations than a private foundation.

Community Foundations – The Charitable Mall

A community foundation is a qualified charity that provides many charitable services and programs to its community. A community foundation often administers donor advised funds. Similar to a mall, a giver can "shop" the available programs within the foundation before choosing to give and can then direct the gift to the specific charitable program or "store" for its use. The giver can make a gift to a community foundation without specific instructions for its use within the scope of the foundation. The community foundation then makes distributions of the funds with regard to the giver's instructions.

The name "community foundation" implies support for the local community and most community foundations provide support in their geographic community. However, an increasing number of community foundations do not have geographic limitations, but consider their "community" to be communities of common interest or faith. There are several self-declared Christian community foundations that support varied programs as decided upon by its board.

One of the often unrecognized benefits to ministries of a faith-based community foundation is the ability to consolidate resources from many givers to allow the foundation to effectively and efficiently meet needs and solve problems on a larger scale than practical for the separate ministries. As ministries' callings and visions of advancing of the kingdom of God become more global, and thus more expensive, this may very well be a way to consolidate resources and increase efficiency in funding the kingdom of God in the future without compromising the integrity of the vision of the ministries involved.

The Building Tools Used to Construct the Legacy

Estate Planning Documents – The Basics

A Will is your declaration of how you want your property distributed at your death. It covers all property that you own in your name that does not have a beneficiary already named, such as life insurance or retirement accounts. It also can leave your wishes for the care of your children and spouse, and can be the document that actually creates trusts, known as testamentary trusts, to further direct the transfer of your estate. Even if you have separate trusts and survivorship beneficiaries, a will can still serve as a catch-all to cover the just-in-case items that may not have made it into these other instruments.

A Durable Power of Attorney allows someone to act on your behalf and conduct business for you, including financial and legal matters, in the event you become physically and/or mentally incapacitated.

A Health Care Power of Attorney (HCPA) is a special kind of durable power of attorney used for health care planning. It allows you to appoint someone else to make health care decisions for you if you become incapable of making that decision, including, if you wish, the decision to refuse intravenous feeding or turn off the respirator if you're in a persistent vegetative state, as well as other medical decisions such as skilled nursing care and surgeries.

A Living Will, also known as a healthcare directive or directive to physicians, is a document that expresses a person's desires and preferences about medical treatment in case he or she becomes unable to communicate these instructions during terminal illness or permanent unconsciousness.

The first living wills helped people who wanted a natural death unattended by artificial life support and other advanced medical techniques. As these documents became more popular and widely available under local laws, they came to include other health care concerns such as tube feeding, resuscitation, and organ donation. While living wills are allowed in all states, they sometimes must follow certain formats and formalities to be effective. If valid, a living will binds health care providers to its instructions as well as provides the family with a clear understanding of a person's true wishes, especially when the person is unable to communicate those wishes and the family most needs to know in order to make crucial decisions.

In recent history, a personal, legal, and political drama unfolded in the debate over the life of Terri Schiavo, a disabled woman who died on March 31, 2005, after having a feeding tube removed 13 days earlier. The argument was between her husband, who argued that she should be allowed to die naturally, and her family, who argued that discontinuing food and fluids was not allowing her die, but ending her life. Terri had no signed healthcare directive or living will. The matter was settled in the courts, not by Terri, because she could no longer communicate her wishes clearly. *I cannot overstate the importance of having your basic estate planning documents in place. If you already have these documents in place, good for you. If not, start the process now.*

A Living Trust, created while you are alive, lets you control the distribution of your estate. You transfer ownership of your property and your assets into the trust. You can serve as the trustee or you can select a person or an institution to be the trustee. If you are the trustee, you will name a successor trustee to manage assets in case you become unable to manage the trust due to incapacitation. The successor trustee will also be responsible for distributing the trust assets at your death. If you change your mind later, you can remove items from the trust or end the trust altogether. One of the advantages of a properly drafted and executed living trust is that it can avoid probate. Because the trust owns the assets, not the deceased, the trustee, not probate, directs the distribution of the assets at death. Only property in the deceased's name must go through probate. One of the downsides of a living trust is that a poorly drawn or unfunded trust can cost you or your estate unnecessary expenses and taxes and endanger your best intentions.

Estate Planning Documents – Advanced Trusts

A Family Trust. Under current US tax law, each US citizen is allowed to pass an unlimited amount of assets in their estate to their US-citizen spouse. This is referred to as the unlimited marital deduction. Also, each citizen is allowed to pass a certain portion of their estate to a non-spouse without estate taxation. This is referred to as the applicable exclusion amount. This "free" portion of their estate is exempt from estate tax due to an offsetting credit against any tax due. At the time of the writing of this book, the estate tax exemption is $5,000,000 for individuals and couples are allowed to combine their exemptions for a total of $10,000,000. This act is set to expire at the end of 2012, reverting back to the 2001 tax law with a $1,000,000 exemption. (For the purposes of the illustrations in this book, unless stated otherwise, all calculations are based on tax law and rates for 2013. For updated calculations and examples, go to www.unleashingthegift.com).

This exemption can only be realized when estate tax is due and the credit is used to offset the tax. So if a giver leaves all of their assets to their spouse at their death, there will be no estate tax due and the credit is not used—and never can be. The value of the assets that were left to the spouse will then be taxable in the spouse's estate, compounding or delaying the process, as the spouse only has their credit to use against potential estate taxes. A credit shelter trust allows a giver to use the value of the credit by creating a taxable estate up to the exemption limit, thereby "sheltering" or preserving the value of their credit. If properly structured, the assets in the credit shelter trust can be used to meet the needs of the surviving spouse and pass on to the family at the spouse's death, but those assets will never be included in the spouse's estate. Because the assets are normally sheltered for the family, this trust is often referred to as a Family Trust.

Example: George and Barbara Davis have an estate valued at $4 million. This includes $2 million in investment assets and $2 million in personal assets, including their home, vacation cabin, and other personal holdings. Without proper estate planning, if George died in 2007 and left all of his assets to Barbara, there would be no estate tax due because of the unlimited marital deduction. However, if Barbara died in 2008 and left all the assets to her children, her children would only receive $3,100,000; the other $900,000 would be the estate tax due.

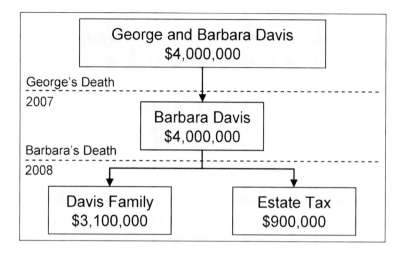

If George and Barbara add a properly-designed and funded Family Trust to their legacy plan, they pass the entire value of their estate to their family without estate taxation.

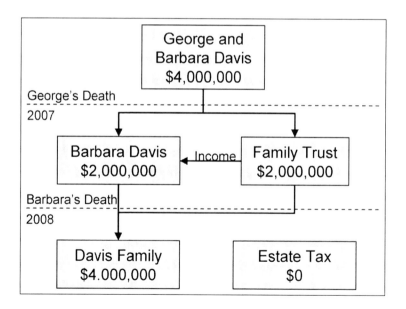

A QTIP Trust is used to protect the value of an estate and protect income for a surviving spouse. A QTIP, or Qualified Terminal Interest Property, trust is used to provide income to a surviving spouse without providing unlimited access to the assets in the trust. The trust provides the income to the surviving spouse for life, and at the death of the spouse, the assets are distributed to the beneficiaries designated in the QTIP trust document. The beneficiary cannot be changed nor can the trust assets be raided, thus protecting the assets for the eventual beneficiaries.

This trust can protect the giver's legacy from a second spouse who may have other desires for the assets. This also has the ability to protect the surviving spouse from children or others who would try to pressure the surviving spouse for money or assets since the surviving spouse only has access to the income, not the assets. This trust is usually established at the giver's death, and the stipulations are irrevocable, so the details need to be fully weighed out and the QTIP trust's design needs to be exact.

An Irrevocable Life Insurance Trust (ILIT), as its name implies, is a trust that is designed to own life insurance and is irrevocably outside the estate. If designed properly, the ILIT will provide needed liquidity at death and the life insurance death benefit will not be subject to estate tax because it is outside the estate. The life insurance proceeds can be used to pay estate taxes, purchase property, create or replace an inheritance to an heir, or provide money for other expenses or needs. It also avoids probate and can avoid claims of creditors of the estate, maintaining privacy and security for the giver.

In order to ensure the assets in the trust stay outside the estate, cash or assets are usually gifted to the trust for the benefit of the named beneficiaries of the trust. The design and implementation of an ILIT can be simple or very complex based on the goals and needs of the giver and should be designed as part of the overall legacy plan. Used properly, the ILIT can be a very efficient and effective part of a well-crafted legacy plan.

A Win-Win Design – The Charitable Remainder Trust with Wealth Replacement Trust. A Charitable Remainder Trust (CRT) has many advantages for the giver, as discussed in a previous section of this book. One of the considerations with a CRT is that the giver is irrevocably giving assets to a trust that will eventually distribute the remainder to a ministry, and not the giver's family. That may be fine for some, but not for others. As its name implies, a Wealth Replacement Trust (WRT) can be used to replace the wealth that is given to the CRT, thereby keeping the value of the inheritance intact for the family to continue the legacy. In other words, the charitable legacy and family legacy are continued together. A Wealth Replacement Trust is typically an Irrevocable Life Insurance Trust funded with life insurance that will replace the value of an asset that is given to a CRT. The name Wealth Replacement Trust is used based on that function.

Example: Marshall and Christina Clark, both 55 years old, own $500,000 of appreciated long-term stock that was given to Marshall by his father ten years ago. His father bought the stock thirty years earlier for $25,000. Because the stock was a gift, Marshall's cost basis for the stock is the same as his father's. The stock pays very little dividends, usually around $5,000, or 1% per year. The Clarks would like to sell the stock and reinvest the proceeds to generate more income. They are assuming that they can get about 5% per year of income by investing the proceeds elsewhere. If the Clarks sold the stock, they would face capital gains tax on the $475,000 gain and reduce the total value of his asset to $390,750 after a 15% Federal capital gains tax and 8% state income tax on the gain. At 5%, the annual first year income would be $19,538. If they spent all the income and maintained the principal, they would leave $390,750 to their children at their death. Given the value of their estate, their estate would have to pay 45% estate tax on the principal, leaving a value to their children of just under $215,000, about 43% of their original value of the stock. They were also hoping to leave something significant to one of their favorite ministries, but the reduction by taxes makes that look very unlikely.

Recap:

Original Value	$500,000
Annual income at 1%	$ 5,000
Tax on sale	$109,250
After-tax proceeds	$390,750
New annual income at 5%	$ 19,538
After-tax value to heirs	$215,000
Percent to heirs	43%
Total Legacy	$215,000

If the Clarks use a Charitable Remainder Trust with a Wealth Replacement Trust, the results change dramatically.

First, the Clarks give the stock to the CRT. The CRT sells the stock with no tax due on the sale. The annual first-year income at 5% is $25,000. The gift of stock to the CRT not only avoids tax on the capital gain, but also generates an income tax deduction of $113,925. This results in a total tax savings of over $41,000. This tax savings can be used to help offset the cost of life insurance purchased for wealth replacement.

As the Clarks are both in excellent health, they are able to purchase a life insurance policy that is designed to pay after Marshall and Christina both pass away. This second-to-die policy will provide $500,000 to replace the value of the gifted stock. The cost for the policy is $3,280/year., which is less than the difference in the annual income of $25,000 with the CRT and $19,538 without the CRT. If they apply the $41,000 to the policy in the first year, the annual payment decreases to $928/year.

They establish the wealth replacement trust and fund it with $41,000 of tax savings and the first year's premium of $928. They are able to gift the total amount to the trust on behalf of their two children without exceeding the annual gifting exclusion by splitting their gift into one gift of $10,482 to each child for Marshall and the same for Christina. The gifts for subsequent years will only total $928. Here is how it works:

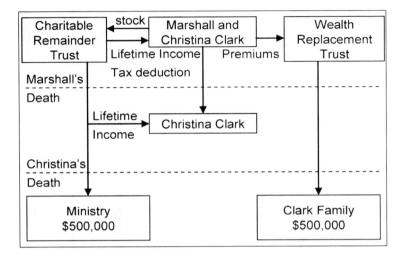

After gifting the annual life insurance premium to the wealth replacement trust, the Clarks are left with $25,000 – $928 = $24,072, over $4,500, 23% more in net income per year than selling the stock outright. Assuming Marshall dies first, Christina still receives the income from the CRT for the rest of her life. At her death, the remaining $500,000 of the assets in the CRT will pay out to the ministry of their choice. Their children will receive the $500,000 death benefit from the Wealth Replacement Trust. The total value of the legacy is $1,000,000.

Here's the summary:

	Outright Sale	CRT with WRT
Original Value	$500,000	$500,000
Annual income at 1%	$ 5,000	$ 5,000
Tax on sale	$109,250	$ 0
After-tax proceeds	$390,750	$500,000
Annual income at 5%	$ 19,538	$ 25,000
Income after insurance	$ 19,538	$ 24,072
Income tax savings	$ 0	$ 41,000
Legacy left to heirs	$215,000	$500,000
Percent to heirs	43%	100%
Legacy left to ministry	$ 0	$500,000
Total Legacy	**$215,000**	**$1,000,000**

By using this win-win combination, Marshall and Christina Clark were able to increase their income, leave the full value of the stock as a legacy to their children, and leave a legacy to their favorite ministry as well. This accomplished all their goals and went beyond their dreams as well.

Not every situation of appreciated assets can be so dramatically solved by using a Charitable Remainder Trust with Wealth Replacement Trust. Some of the key variables are the income, capital gain, and estate tax rate; the amount of the gift; the age, health and insurability of the giver; and the income requirements of the giver. A valuable tool to be sure, but not a one-size-fits-all by any means, and it must fit with the giver's overall legacy plan for the optimal benefit.

The Contractors – The Professionals that Design and Build the Legacy Plan

Whenever a giver endeavors to build and leave a legacy, just like building a custom-designed home, the giver needs a team of skilled craftsmen to help design and implement that plan. Some of the roles on that team are listed below and one person could take on multiple roles based on their expertise and licenses. This is not an all-inclusive list, but represents the core group of "contractors" needed to build a lasting legacy plan.

The Accountant

A Certified Public Accountant (CPA) helps the giver plan for and manage the tax ramifications of their legacy plan. The CPA is also the one who can give *specific* tax advice on the taxation or deductibility of a specific tool, strategy, or course of action. Some CPAs operate as generalists; some specialize in business tax, some in estate tax, and some in both. The adage in construction is, "Measure twice; cut once." This is especially true with sophisticated planning using irrevocable trusts, which yield irrevocable decisions, and the CPA is a critical member of the legacy planning team.

The Attorney

An Estate Planning Attorney works with the giver to draft the legacy planning documents, trusts, etc. Depending on the level of complexity of the legacy plan, the giver will often need an attorney who specializes in advanced estate planning and has experience drafting, executing, and funding complex trust arrangements, both traditional and charitable.

The Underwriter

An Insurance Underwriter works with the giver to design and implement any life insurance or long-term care insurance solutions for the legacy plan. An independent underwriter can survey multiple companies to find the best company with the best product that best fits the giver's needs, given their financial resources, health, family history, cash flow, and other criteria that determine cost and appropriateness of different insurance-based solutions. A true risk management craftsman, the skilled independent underwriter can help minimize cost while maximizing the benefit for the need.

The Investment Manager

An Investment Manager helps the giver choose investment products that fit the giver's income needs, required rate of return, and risk tolerance, and helps the giver purchase those products. The independent investment manager can access a range of investment options with multiple companies to custom design an investment strategy that will best meet the objectives of the different parts of the legacy plan, including lifetime income, retirement plan management, trust asset management, etc. They can also help evaluate any existing investment programs and integrate them in the overall legacy plan. Making sure the investment portfolios meet the needs of the overall plan is crucial to the success of the plan.

Other Advisors

The Gift Planner, also known as a Development Officer, usually works for a ministry. They have expertise in designing planned giving systems and programs, such as the pooled income fund, charitable gift annuity, and charitable trusts. They advise the ministry and assist the giver with implementing various types of current and deferred gifts and provide educational illustrations of how those gifts might work for the giver and benefit the ministry. In addition, the gift planner can help make sure that the gift is directed within the ministry in accordance with the giver's preferences as much as possible.

A Commercial Banker can assist the giver in any banking or lending they may need in managing any business restructuring, purchase, or sale of the giver's business interests.

A Real Estate Broker can assist the giver in any real estate purchases or sales. Some real estate brokers (or their agents) handle residential, some handle commercial, and some handle both.

A Certified Business Appraiser can help the giver determine the value of any business interests for sale or gifting purposes. With special expertise in valuation adjustments, the business appraiser helps make sure any gift values are valid for valuation or deduction purposes.

The General Contractor – The Legacy Advisor

The legacy advisor is the giver's representative who oversees the legacy plan design and implementation and coordinates all of the professional services that the giver needs to build and implement the designed legacy plan. Similar to the general contractor for a custom-built home, the legacy advisor has expertise and familiarity in all the aspects of the process.

The legacy advisor often takes one or more of the contractor roles mentioned above while keeping all the details and actions of the planning process moving together, each at the right time and place. In order to help the giver unleash the gift of giving in building and leaving a legacy for the giver's family and for the kingdom of God, the legacy advisor must have a unique skill set and characteristics, including operating as a legacy advisor as his or her calling from God. The legacy advisor should be an expert in:

- Knowing the heart of the giver. That means asking the question behind the question, digging deeper than surface level, and helping the giver discover their own calling, vision, dreams and goals, and being the valued confidant to partner together to accomplish that vision.
- Knowing the value of the ministry. Not just knowing about the ministry, but knowing the heart and vision of the ministry to help mesh the vision of the min-

istry with the vision of the giver in a practical and meaningful way.

- Applying the word of God to situations. As has already been discussed, many givers do not know what the Bible says about wealth, vision, purpose, and calling. The legacy advisor must be skilled in the word of God concerning giving and wealth to assist and disciple the giver through the process as needed.
- Designing and implementing the blueprints (the legacy plan) to ensure that the irrevocable finished product accomplishes the goals and dreams of the giver.
- The use of legacy building supplies (forms of giving) and tools; not just the technical aspects, but their functionality and how they work together.
- Assembling the team of subcontractors and understanding the expertise needed from each member to oversee, coordinate, and implement the legacy plan.

Chapter 5

Legacy Plans In Action: Profiles of Givers

> *Dear friends, do you think you'll get any-*
> *where in this if you learn all the right words*
> *but never do anything? Does merely talking*
> *about faith indicate that a person really has*
> *it? For instance, you come upon an old friend*
> *dressed in rags and half-starved and say,*
> *"Good morning, friend! Be clothed in Christ!*
> *Be filled with the Holy Spirit!" and walk off*
> *without providing so much as a coat or a*
> *cup of soup—where does that get you? Isn't*
> *it obvious that God-talk without God-acts is*
> *outrageous nonsense?*
>
> *I can already hear one of you agreeing*
> *by saying, "Sounds good. You take care of*
> *the faith department, I'll handle the works*
> *department." Not so fast. You can no more*
> *show me your works apart from your faith*
> *than I can show you my faith apart from my*
> *works. Faith and works, works and faith, fit*
> *together hand in glove.*
>
> *James 2:14-18 (Message)*

Disclaimer: As with all of the examples in this book, the names and details are ficticious and are based upon assumptions that may or may not apply to your specific situation. They are used as concept illustrations for instructional purposes only. Always consult competent professional advice for your individual situation.

The Widow Who Traded Sorrow For Joy

Kathleen Morgan is a sweet 70-year-old widow with a heart of gold. She has such a simple joy in all she does. Her husband, Lloyd, died a few years ago after a lengthy battle with cancer. Kathleen's only child, Debra, is her best friend and shopping buddy. Debra is a successful entrepreneur and lives several states away, but they stay close by phone and see each other when they can.

Many years ago, Debra and Kathleen were not on very good terms. During her headstrong teenage years, Debra moved out of her parents' home and moved in with a much older boyfriend with a rather sordid past. After months of arguing and break-ups with even more fragile reunions, Debra and her boyfriend had a major fight that turned violent, leaving Debra in the hospital recovering from wounds and broken bones for several days. After eating a lot of crow, Debra confided in her mother that she had been physically abused for some time. She knew it was bad, but did not have the strength to swallow her pride and return home and felt she had nowhere else to go. Debra has never married nor has any children. Most of the time she has the same joy as Kathleen, but the memories of the abuse still linger.

Out of Kathleen's heart of gold and her empathy due to her daughter's experience, she has always been a supporter of the Heavenly Haven battered women's shelter since it opened nearly five years ago. Founded by several women in her church, the Heavenly Haven has given battered women the compassion and safety they need as well as a discipleship program to help them develop in their walk with the Lord. Kathleen volunteers as a Bible study leader several times a month and makes regular financial contributions.

Before Kathleen's husband died, in an attempt to get all of his affairs in order, he transferred a piece of land into Kathleen's name. The land was rented to a farmer for hay for a small amount of money, but that was years ago and only a portion of the land is still farmed. The value on the land is around $750,000 and the annual rent is $3,600, less than ½%. When Lloyd bought the land, he got a really good deal on it —$5,000 for the 60 acres. Most of the land in that area used to be farmland; now it is full of schools, neighborhoods, and boutique shops. The taxes alone on the land are more than the rent. Kathleen has had several people call her and ask her to sell, but up until now she has held on to it for sentimental reasons and the daunting potential tax on the sale.

While visiting at the Heavenly Haven, she heard someone mention a new program they had started to help raise money for expansion—a Charitable Gift Annuity. Once Julie, the Heavenly Haven's new gift planner, explained the details, Kathleen knew this was what she had been looking for. She was doing okay financially, but she wanted to be able to do more—more travel, more for her daughter, and more for the Heavenly Haven, and even more to be protected in case she should ever need medical care in the future. She had looked at long-term care insurance, but at her age, it was quite expensive and she could not justify spending the money on it.

In a few weeks, Kathleen and Julie had worked out all the details. Kathleen would give the land to the Heavenly Haven in exchange for a Charitable Gift Annuity (CGA.) The CGA would provide her with an annual payment of $45,750 for the rest of her life, of which over $28,300 was tax-free, and she would get a charitable tax deduction of nearly $300,000. Not only that, she was making a meaningful gift to the Heavenly Haven in the process!

After getting the good news, she realized she had enough income to purchase the long-term care insurance she had been putting off. After discussing all of this with Debra, Debra took off time from work to help Kathleen with all the details. During their time together, Kathleen mentioned that this would reduce Debra's inheritance. After a minute or two of reassuring her mother that she was well-taken care of with her career, she told her mom that the gift to help other women who were going through what she had been through was the greatest gift her mother could ever give her. When the two of them stopped crying together, Kathleen was at peace about her decision. So they moved on to the next important detail: planning their next trip together—a shopping spree in Chicago—Kathleen's treat!

Kathleen exchanged her low income asset and potential taxes for increased income that she can never outlive, an income tax deduction, a spreading of the capital gains taxes, and made a meaningful gift for the Heavenly Haven ministry. *She truly traded her sorrow for joy!*

A Gift of Life After Death

Robert and Cathy Alvarez met in high school, fell in love, were married, and had four children. Their life seems typical, but their lifestyle is anything but typical. Robert is the state director of a Christian recovery program for teens and adults with substance abuse addictions and Cathy works with him on staff.

After years of seeing the number of lives that have been changed through the power of the Gospel and a disciplined lifestyle, Robert and Cathy want to make sure that when they "retire to heaven" that they are able to make sure the ministry will continue on without them. There has been steady growth, sometimes faster than Robert and Cathy can keep up with, but sometimes the growth is faster than the finances. Robert hates to slow down; "Blowin' and goin' for Jesus!" is his favorite saying. They thought about starting a monthly savings account to leave to the ministry after they retired to heaven.

After attending a ministry workshop on giving, Robert and Cathy decided to do something about their wish to leave a legacy with the ministry. They decided to have the ministry purchase a life insurance policy for each of them and they would agree to pay the premiums as a gift to the ministry. This ministry-owned life insurance would provide $500,000 after Robert and Cathy's death for about $500 per month, which was about what Robert and Cathy had already decided to give before they went to the workshop. The return on their money was more than they had thought.

When they presented their idea to the board, it was so well-received that several of the board members decided to explore the same option for themselves and to offer this to all of their key donors and partners. They even decided that the board would pay the premiums on Robert and Cathy's policy if they would agree to increase it to $1,000,000. The chairman of the board told Robert and Cathy that it would take a lot more money than that to ever replace all the work they did for the ministry, but that was a good start.

Within the next few months, the board hired a gift planner to help Robert and Cathy with all of the new deferred gifts they were setting up and the board asked them to make plans to launch a full planned giving campaign. Robert and Cathy know that they are giving the men and women they minister to a new life, and they named their new program, "Giving the Gift of Life After Death."

The Oil That Would Not Run Out

Ray Jackson is a Texan. He's very adamant about that point. Yes, he's a patriotic American, but only after being a Texan. He despises two things—taxes and the devil. He seems to lump the two of them together regularly in conversation. Ray is in his early 70's and he pays too much in taxes. Way too much! He has more money than he needs and lives a fairly modest lifestyle, especially after his wife of 50 years died a few years ago. He has two children that got into the oil business with him and now they run the whole operation. Ray has already transferred the business operation over to them, but he still has a few oil wells that are in his name from his wildcatting days.

Ray, who started with nothing out of high school, worked his way up in the oil business in Texas, doing any job he could get from fireman to toolpusher to foreman to truck driver to gopher. After a couple of speculative investments with his savings into wildcat drilling, one of the wells hit big. Things grew to Ray running his own drilling company. His sons have taken over all of that now, and Ray has a company pension for life. The wells that are still in his name are sending him regular income that he does not need. That would make most people happy, but not Ray. Remember, he hates taxes. Yes, his savings account is growing, but he does not need the money and he cannot stand the thought of paying all those unnecessary taxes! He would just give the oil wells to his sons, but he has already used up his lifetime gifts on the business and even had to pay gift taxes. He says it's the first time in nearly thirty years that he almost cussed (that's Texan for cursed).

His only "saving grace" for taxes are his contributions to an evangelistic association ministry that he has supported for years. When Ray was in his earlier days, he was not exactly saved. He did not even know anyone that was. He cussed, smoked, and drank. He had a guy at work invite him to a meeting with this ministry. After cussing a little, he agreed to go to the meeting. During the meeting, still not completely sober, the Holy Spirit began getting through to Ray's heart. He walked the aisle, accepted the Lord, and was completely delivered from alcohol and cigarettes. He had to work for a while on the cussing, but eventually got that one, too. Ever since then, Ray has supported this ministry which has grown into a worldwide outreach.

Unfortunately, as a result of his previous lifestyle, he is completely uninsurable. That makes him almost as mad as taxes, since he knows the devil stole those years from him and now he cannot transfer the rest of his estate to his sons without more taxes and cannot even buy the life insurance to pay the estate taxes.

One day, he attended a partner meeting for the ministry. They had a speaker who taught on Biblical Finance and funding the kingdom of God. Some of the things the speaker mentioned got Ray's attention, especially the whole idea of legacy planning instead of just estate planning. He had paid a firm in town over $50,000 years ago for his estate plan and it still was not what he wanted, especially after he paid the gift taxes.

After the meeting, Ray called the speaker. As it turned out, Brent Brooks, the speaker, was a legacy advisor who specialized in working with givers like Ray who wanted to help the kingdom of God and hated taxes and the devil. Ray set up a meeting with Brent and hired him on the spot.

After going through the legacy planning process, Ray realized that he had already accomplished most of his goals, and that he really wanted to do something more for the evangelistic ministry. Brent explained about a Deferred Inheritance Trust, also known as a CLAT, where Ray could lend the oil wells to the ministry, let the ministry receive the income, and then pass the oil wells to his sons estate-tax free. This seemed amazing! No more unnecessary income taxes? No more estate taxes? And help the ministry? This is what Ray had been looking for!

The value of Ray's wells were $4,000,000. They were generating annual income of $400,000. Brent showed Ray that he could gift the wells to the CLAT, the CLAT would hold the wells for 13 years and pay the income to the ministry, and would then pass the wells to his sons at no gift or estate taxes. If Ray passed away before the time was up, at the end of the 13 years, his sons would receive the wells free of any gift or estate tax. Ray had never been happier. By working with Brent, he was able to beat the tax man and give money to the ministry and still get the oil wells to his sons. It was a great plan!

Tom and Dorothy Taylor: Designed to Give

Tom (59) and Dorothy (58) work together in their own successful business, Taylor Designs, a commercial upholstery fabric designer and manufacturer. Tom began working with his father in the company, Taylor Fabrics, when he graduated from college. Starting out in sales, Tom would call on local and regional furniture manufacturers and reupholsters, Taylor Designs' core clients, to show the designs for the new season. In a short time, Tom was able to expand the company's sales into a multi-state territory.

After he married Dorothy, his college sweetheart who had majored in graphic design, Tom and Dorothy began Taylor Designs, a division of Taylor Fabrics that focused on innovative custom designs for commercial furniture. After years of great exertion and limited results, a successful meeting with an airline executive led to their first major contract. The airline was refurbishing all of their flying club rooms nationwide and wanted a uniform furniture upholstery design that would be unique. This contract gave Taylor Designs the momentum it needed to become a key player in the industry and led to greater and greater successes.

With Tom's father retiring and giving him the family business and with the bulk of Taylor Fabrics' revenue now coming from custom design work, Tom renamed the business Taylor Designs. Over twenty years later, Tom and Dorothy have grown Taylor Designs into a multi-million dollar custom design and manufacturing firm with several offices throughout the country.

Tom and Dorothy have four adult children, Paul, Lydia, Daniel, and Elizabeth. They are all married and have their own families and remain very close, always managing to spend Mother's Day and Christmas with Tom and Dorothy. Lydia followed in her mother's footsteps and pursued a career in design. After a few years in the New York fashion world, she returned home and helped in the family business, growing the custom design line to include corporate wall covering for specialty meeting rooms.

Now Tom and Dorothy are contemplating their future, wanting to spend less time running the business and more time pursuing other interests, and are becoming increasingly concerned about legacy. The business has matured and grown into a substantial operation. Bill, the company's director of operations, provides the day-to-day stability of the company while Lydia is developing more and more creativity and a desire to expand. None of the other children are involved in the business nor show any desire to start, each pursuing their own diverse careers.

Tom and Dorothy have always been active in their church and have gone on some short-term missions trips, but the demands of running the business has kept them close to the helm. They would like to become more involved in ministry activities and leave a legacy of something other than just a business. Tom and Dorothy's pastor, Ben Whitney, recently recommended they attend a business person Bible study with some other business professionals. Although they have always tried to honor God with their wealth, they never really felt connected, almost as if their financial position kept them separated and isolated. When they attended this Bible study, they found many other successful business people with the same feelings: isolation, loneliness, and even rejection, somehow feeling that God was not pleased with their material wealth. Through the study, they begin to see how God designed the whole idea of wealth, that it is his desire that His people be blessed and steward that blessing to be a blessing to others. When the study turned to different gifts, they saw how their gifts of creative craftsmanship were a gift from God to use to bring glory to Him, and that their lifelong desire to help others financially was actually the gift of giving. All this time they had thought their money isolated them from God; now they realized their money was to help them fulfill His calling on their life.

At the conclusion of the Bible study, Tom and Dorothy, along with their other new friends, committed themselves to leave a lasting legacy based on their giftings. They had spent nearly all of their life building their business; they were now ready to transition out of the day-to-day operation of their business and commit the rest of their lives to passing on their gifts of entrepreneurial leadership, craftsmanship, and giving to their children, and operate more in their newly-discovered gifts to make a personal difference for the kingdom of God. Not knowing exactly where to start, they met with their friend, Sue Miller, the director of the ministry that had led their past short-term missions trip. She referred them to a legacy advisor to help them discover their legacy goals and develop a plan to accomplish their goals.

Both excited and a little apprehensive about developing their legacy plan, they met with Josh Landis, the legacy advisor Sue recommended. In the first meeting with Josh, they confirmed their decision to transition from the day-to-day business life to pursue a more significant role in ministry work for the rest of their lives and pass that significance, their legacy, to their children. After over two hours of talking, Josh said that the next step was to conduct a Legacy Retreat, a time for introspection and creativity that would direct the planning for their future. Tom suggested they meet at their mountain cabin because it was one of their favorite places to get away from the distractions and pressures of the daily grind. Josh ended the meeting by giving Tom and Dorothy a Legacy Retreat questionnaire booklet that they were to fill out individually and return to Josh for his review before the retreat.

During the Legacy Retreat, Josh led Tom and Dorothy through a series of intertwined discussions based on their questionnaires, exploring areas of their value system and their individual gifts that they had never considered. They were very surprised that so little time was spent on discussing the financial details of their business, their assets, their estate planning documents, their tax situation, and other important, yet mundane, details. Soon they began to see how their values and giftings should drive those details instead of being driven by them. They began seeing how the financial aspect of their wealth, although important, should not be the first consideration in their planning. They realized that the spiritual, emotional, and relational purpose of their wealth was much more important. They discussed their views on the purpose of wealth, their perspective of treating their children equally versus fairly, their view of God, and their passion for helping orphans in Kenya. At the end of the two-day retreat, they felt exhausted and empowered at the same time. They were finally starting to gain clarity and purpose for their lives and were more motivated than ever to complete their legacy plan.

Josh gave them more homework to do before their next meeting. Based on the Legacy Retreat, Josh helped them create a Family Legacy Letter of Intent, a document that memorializes how they obtained their wealth, their beliefs concerning life's meaning and their purpose and calling, and their responsibilities to their heirs and to others.

During the next meeting, they reviewed the letter as well as confirmed a prioritized list of their goals for their Family Legacy Plan. Their goals, in order, are:

1. Transfer Taylor Designs to their daughter, Lydia, within the next five years without being devastated by capital gains or estate taxes.

2. At their deaths, leave their other three children an inheritance equal to the value of the business that they want to leave to Lydia.

3. Establish financial independence by maintaining a $350,000 after-tax income for life, indexed for inflation.
4. Create a charitable fund to allow Tom and Dorothy to actively make a significant difference for the orphanages in Kenya.
5. Pass on a legacy of passion for God and caring for others to their children.
6. Minimize current income taxes.
7. Eliminate all capital gains and estate taxes.

After confirming their goals, they provide Josh with all of their business, legal, financial, and tax information relating to their current situation as well as all the details of their current estate planning. They now realize how daunting their goals appear and how ill-prepared they are for this transition, but Josh assures them that he will work together with them along with their current advisors as they design their new Family Legacy Plan to accomplish as many of their goals as possible.

After meeting with Brenda Price, Tom and Dorothy's accountant, and Will Chambers, their attorney, Josh meets with Tom and Dorothy to go over the details of the Family Legacy Plan. First, Josh shows them what would happen to their legacy with their existing plan.

Tom and Dorothy's Assets

Personal Holdings

Personal residence......................................$1,250,000

Mountain cabin $840,000

Other personal property $385,000

Total personal holdings $2,475,000

Business Holdings
Taylor Designs (basis: $240,000) $27,500,000

Retirement and Investment Assets
Tom's 401(k) $1,230,000
Dorothy's 401(k) $1,439,000
Savings, CDs, etc. $174,000
Investment portfolio $838,000
Total retirement and investment assets $3,681,000

Debt (mortgage on personal residence) $400,000

Net Worth **$33,256,000**

Life Insurance
Tom's universal life policy
      (personally owned) $2,000,000
Dorothy's term policy
      (personally owned) $1,000,000

Gross estate **$36,256,000**

Gross estate at life expectancy **$98,453,000**

Federal estate tax* **$43,854,000**

Net inheritance to heirs **$55,599,000**

Percent to heirs **55.46%**

Total annual income at retirement** **$184,050**

*Assumes Tom and Dorothy's death in 2027, Dorothy's death in 2030. Debt retired and estate assets grow at 5%.

**Retirement income is 5% of investment assets, compounded at 9%, assuming 4% inflation.

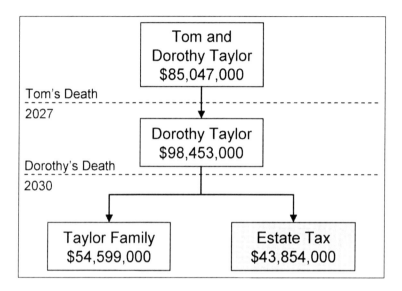

The review of their existing planning was eye-opening to say the least. First, their ability to maintain their financial independence goal was not possible with their current situation. The cash flow of the business allowed them a great deal of financial freedom, but now they needed to hire additional staff to replace the work that Lydia and Bill currently do. It never occurred to them that they had no plan to pay themselves when they were no longer working at the company. Yes, they had saved some money for retirement, but most of their savings had been reinvested into growing the company. If that were not enough bad news, the taxation at their death would mean the company would have to be sold just to pay the taxes. All they had worked for could not even sustain them, let alone survive to sustain their dreams for the next generation. They realized they had spent so much time and energy making the company thrive at the expense of planning for their ability to survive without the company or its ability to survive without them. Feeling more than a little anxious and guilty, they wondered how they could have been so short-sighted. Now their goals seemed more than daunting; they seemed hopeless.

After what seemed like a painful eternity, Josh went on to the new plan. After going through a series of charts, diagrams, and explanations, Tom and Dorothy began to feel the heaviness slowly lift. This new Family Legacy Plan, to their amazement, accomplishes all of their goals. Not one or two, but all seven! It was just what they had wanted!

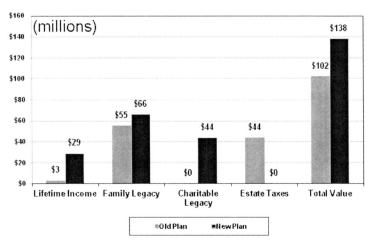

This new Family Legacy Plan enabled them to not only survive without the company, but for them and the company to thrive well into the next generation. And, they would be free to pursue their ministry endeavors with the orphanages in Kenya within the next five years without worrying about the financial provision to do so. There was even a plan for taking care of the company in case something happened to Lydia. Josh, working with Brenda, their accountant, and Will, their attorney, had managed to do it all.

Once Josh finished explaining the details of the plan, Tom and Dorothy actually understood the main details of the plan, something they had never been able to do before. Until now, all of the legal and tax aspects of their planning had been so confusing. No wonder it did not make sense before—it was all rules, numbers, and graphs that explained what they could not do. Now they were seeing that it was all tied to what was important to them, their goals they had discovered. In the past, they had never wanted to even deal with the future; now they were ready to run to it!

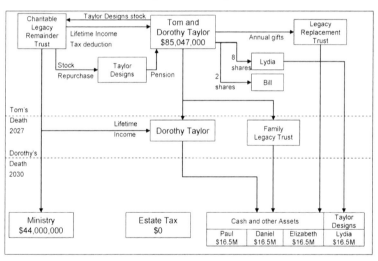

One of the most rewarding steps of this process was the Taylor family meeting. Gathering all the children together with their spouses, the Taylors explained to their children about their experiences over the past several months. With Josh's help, Tom and Dorothy presented each of their children with an overview of their Family Legacy Plan, including their Family Legacy Vision, the letter they had designed with Josh to memorialize how they built their legacy, and how they desired for it to continue in future generations.

Finally, after the months of preparation and work, Tom and Dorothy were able to clearly articulate their goals, their giftings, and their desire for their legacy. They explained and discussed the steps of their Family Legacy Plan, especially the end result after Tom and Dorothy had finished their work in this life. They were very encouraged to see the excitement, and in some cases, relief that their children shared over the plan, especially the sense of unity over working together to oversee the continuation of the Family Legacy Foundation, Tom and Dorothy's vehicle to pass on a legacy of passion for God and caring for others to their children.

The next few weeks were exciting. Tom and Dorothy were very energized. All the years of work and sacrifice were actually going to pay off. After meeting with Josh and Will, they drafted all the legal documents necessary and began repositioning assets as outlined in the plan.

When all the details were finally in place, Tom and Dorothy set up a meeting with their pastor to catch him up on their progress. They began telling him about their desire to work with orphanages in Kenya. Pastor Whitney recommended they contact a missionary pastor in Kenya, Pastor Wayne Powers. Pastor Powers and his wife, Carol, had been in Kenya for over twenty years and were overseeing the growth of several orphanages in Kenya and the surrounding countries.

After a short trip to Kenya, Tom and Dorothy began making the necessary arrangements to begin the transition of Taylor Designs to the control of their daughter, Lydia, the new Chief Executive Officer, and Bill, the new Chief Operations Officer. Tom and Dorothy would maintain positions on the board, but were quickly turning over the day-to-day responsibilities to their new leadership team. This transition was challenging, but very rewarding, and moved much more efficiently than they had anticipated.

Even though Tom and Dorothy's professional career with Taylor Designs was coming to a close, they felt more energized than ever in their new career as professional legacy builders! The extra income available as a result of their Family Legacy Plan gave them the resources they needed to live very comfortably as well as fund the projects they were taking on with the orphanages in Kenya. They really felt that they were operating in their giftings as God had uniquely designed them: designed to give.

Closing Thoughts

Don't fool yourself into thinking that you are a listener when you are anything but, letting the Word go in one ear and out the other. Act on what you hear! Those who hear and don't act are like those who glance in the mirror, walk away, and two minutes later have no idea who they are, what they look like. But whoever catches a glimpse of the revealed counsel of God—the free life!—even out of the corner of his eye, and sticks with it, is no distracted scatterbrain but a man or woman of action. That person will find delight and affirmation in the action.

James 1:22-25 (The Message)

Go and Do

Proper decisive action leads to victory but inaction never will. Procrastination is not a virtue. After reading this book, you have enough information to begin building a lasting legacy for your ministry and assist givers in building and leaving their legacy.

You have learned about:

1. The necessity for unleashing the gift of giving.
2. The unique needs of a giver.

3. The value of a ministry and a giver working together around a common vision.
4. The ministry's need to assess its legacy capital.
5. Tools used to create a successful legacy plan.
6. Ways a giver can plan their legacy that will provide needed capital to a ministry, often resulting in more capital for the giver also.
7. The ministry and giver's need to work with a legacy advisor to bring the process together.

The best way to implement these learnings is as unique as your ministry. The first step should be the same for every ministry: seek God. Take time, as much as you need, and maybe more than you think you need, and seek God's will concerning His role for your ministry in helping to unleash the gift of giving, both to benefit your ministry and to benefit the legacy of the giver.

Here are some general ideas that could help you develop your action plan.

1-on-1 Meetings

Meet with one of your ministry's main supporters for lunch or coffee, both husband and wife if they are married. Share with them what you have learned in this book. Ask them for their help in better understanding the needs of the giver, including their needs. Be transparent. Share your vision with them. Tell them what God showed you when you went to seek Him concerning this. Get their feedback and ask them for their help in building your ministry's legacy by unleashing the gift of giving.

Private Briefings

Take the learnings you have gained and share it. Gather a small group of couples from your ministry's main supporters and share with them what you have learned. Teach them about the tools. Share the stories of the legacy plans in action. Have follow-up meetings to enlist their feedback and ask them for their help in building your ministry's legacy by unleashing the gift of giving.

Vision Meetings

Host a vision meeting dinner. Invite a group of your ministry's supporters and their friends as well as those who you know that might become supporters. Share the impact you are making today and your vision for future growth. Share some of the learnings from this book: the reasons people give, the ways people give, the stories of the legacy plans in action. Give them an opportunity to meet with you later to discuss ways of working together to fulfill the vision.

Final Word—Unleash The Gift!

Dear brothers and sisters, I close my letter with these last words: Be joyful. Grow to maturity. Encourage each other. Live in harmony and peace. Then the God of love and peace will be with you.

II Cor. 13:11 (NLT)

With your new understanding of the interdependence between the ministry and the giver, you are in the ideal position to help unleash the gift of giving. Unleashing the gift of giving is the key to building and leaving a legacy for the kingdom of God. It is my heartfelt prayer that God would work through you to unleash the gift of giving to further His kingdom.

If you are interested in working with a legacy advisor to help facilitate your unleashing the gift of giving, I would be glad to discuss the opportunity with you. You can contact me at my office by phone at 336-499-4999. Just tell my staff that you are a ministry that is ready to unleash the gift of giving and they will set up a time for us to discuss your situation over the phone.

Appendix: The Capital Assessment

Spiritual Capital

Vision

Do I personally have this capital in my life? ❏Y ❏N To what degree?

_____

_____

Do we need this capital in the ministry? ❏Y ❏N To what degree?

_____

_____

Do we have this capital in the ministry? ❏Y ❏N To what degree?

_____

_____

Do I want the ministry to pass this capital on as a legacy?
❏Y ❏N To what degree?

_____

_____

Integrity

Do I personally have this capital in my life? ❏Y ❏N To what degree?

_____

_____

Do we need this capital in the ministry? ❏Y ❏N To what degree?

_____

_____

Do we have this capital in the ministry? ❏Y ❏N To what degree?

_____

_____

Do I want the ministry to pass this capital on as a legacy?
❏Y ❏N To what degree?

_____

_____

Mandates

Do I personally have this capital in my life? ❏Y ❏N To what degree?

_____

_____

Do we need this capital in the ministry? ❏Y ❏N To what degree?

_____

_____

Do we have this capital in the ministry? ❏Y ❏N To what degree?

_____

_____

Do I want the ministry to pass this capital on as a legacy?
❏Y ❏N To what degree?

_____

_____

Ministry Gifting: Apostle, prophet, evangelist, pastor, teaching, missionary

Do I personally have this capital in my life? ❑Y ❑N To what degree?

_____

_____

Do we need this capital in the ministry? ❑Y ❑N To what degree?

_____

_____

Do we have this capital in the ministry? ❑Y ❑N To what degree?

_____

_____

Do I want the ministry to pass this capital on as a legacy?
❑Y ❑N To what degree?

_____

_____

Functional Gifting: Helps, leadership, administration, craftsmanship, service, giving, music, knowledge, wisdom, prayer, hospitality, mercy, exhortation

Do I personally have this capital in my life? ❑Y ❑N To what degree?

_____

_____

Do we need this capital in the ministry? ❑Y ❑N To what degree?

_____

_____

Do we have this capital in the ministry? ❑Y   ❑N To what degree?

_____

_____

Do I want the ministry to pass this capital on as a legacy?
❑Y   ❑N To what degree?

_____

_____

Human Capital

<u>Leadership</u>

Do I personally have this capital in my life? ❑Y ❑N To what degree?

_____

Do we need this capital in the ministry? ❑Y ❑N To what degree?

_____

Do we have this capital in the ministry? ❑Y ❑N To what degree?

_____

Do I want the ministry to pass this capital on as a legacy? ❑Y ❑N To what degree?

_____

<u>Intellectual Capacity:</u> Learning and renewing

Do I personally have this capital in my life? ❑Y ❑N To what degree?

_____

Do we need this capital in the ministry? ❑Y ❑N To what degree?

_____

Do we have this capital in the ministry? ❑Y ❑N To what degree?

_____

Do I want the ministry to pass this capital on as a legacy? ❑Y ❑N To what degree?

_____

Physical Capacity

Do I personally have this capital in my life? ❑Y ❑N To what degree?

_____

Do we need this capital in the ministry? ❑Y ❑N To what degree?

_____

Do we have this capital in the ministry? ❑Y ❑N To what degree?

_____

Do I want the ministry to pass this capital on as a legacy? ❑Y ❑N To what degree?

_____

Spiritual Capacity

Do I personally have this capital in my life? ❑Y ❑N To what degree?

_____

Do we need this capital in the ministry? ❑Y ❑N To what degree?

_____

Do we have this capital in the ministry? ❑Y ❑N To what degree?

_____

About The Author

Rusty Russell, CFP*, is a CERTIFIED FINANCIAL PLANNER™ professional and founder of a legacy planning firm located in Winston-Salem, North Carolina. Rusty, a native of North Carolina, has a Bachelor's degree in Chemistry from Furman University and a Master's degree in Management from the University of Southern California.

In 1995, after nine years as a US Army officer, Rusty decided to pursue the financial planning field with a national financial planning company. In 1998, Rusty founded his own firm. Rusty specializes in family legacy planning, a customized process that helps families build and leave a family and ministry legacy. He guides clients through a disciplined process that facilitates taking advantage of the opportunities and avoiding the potential pitfalls inherent in their financial success. This results in financial independence today and a lasting legacy for generations to come.

Rusty has served as a faculty member for the Guilford College Certified Financial Planner program, teaching retirement and estate planning fundamentals to CFP® certification candidates, and as a fellow with Life Christian University, teaching a course to ministry students on Biblical finance. He also teaches professional continuing education courses in the areas of wealth management and business succession. Rusty and his wife, Michele, have four children and are active in leadership at Agape Faith Church in Clemmons, North Carolina.

CPSIA information can be obtained at www.ICGtesting.com
Printed in the USA
BVOW031458141212

307891BV00001B/2/P

9 781936 750672